Lorne B. Hemming

July 17/86

ACCORDING TO *Hakluyt*

According

By the same author/*Last Voyage of the Unicorn*, *The Ghost Ship*

Hakluyt

Tales of adventure and exploration

Delbert A. Young

Clarke, Irwin & Company Limited/Toronto, Vancouver 1973

ISBN 0-7720-0587-7

1 2 3 4 5 6 78 77 76 75 74 73

Printed in Canada

Contents

VOYAGES TO THE SOUTH ATLANTIC

VOYAGES AROUND THE GLOBE

Introduction

Recently a speaker asked an audience of 100 educated persons this question: "How many of you know who Richard Hakluyt was?"

To his astonishment, only four hands went up. Richard Hakluyt contributed more to English letters, and has had more effect on English writing, than any other man who ever lived, with the possible exception of Shakespeare. In contrast to the few in the audience who knew who Hakluyt was, practically all had read about Martin Frobisher, John Davis, John Hawkins, Francis Drake, Walter Raleigh, Humphrey Gilbert and other Elizabethan seamen. Their knowledge of those famous English sailors had come to them via a host of other writers. What none of them realized is that writers, particularly historical writers, have for four centuries been using Hakluyt's massive work, *The Principall Navigations, Voiages and Discoveries of the English Nation,* more popularly known as *Hakluyt's Voyages,* as an essential source for their own writings.

Richard Hakluyt was a lanky clergyman who travelled, mostly on horseback, the length and breadth of England, not once but many times, in a never-ending quest for the stories, the "I-was-there" accounts of the Elizabethan seamen who, during the last half of the sixteenth century, laid the foundations of the British Empire and changed the history of the western world.

He was born circa 1553, the son of a London leather merchant—his father is described as Richard of the Skinners' Company. Both Hakluyt senior and his wife died in 1557 (probably of the plague, since they died within days of one another), leaving young Richard, three brothers and two sisters orphaned. In the will of Richard the Skinner we find these words: "To my cousin Richard Hackelett

40s in money." This statement is closely followed by another: "Cousin Richard Hackelett overseer: to be aiding, assisting, and comforting my said executrix, he to have the 40s for his pains." In Tudor England the terms "cousin" and "nephew" appear to have been interchangeable. Cousin Richard was in fact the elder Hakluyt's nephew.

The dying man could not know how important to England's literature, and her history, those few words inserted into his will were to become. When the executrix, his widow, died shortly after her husband, his nephew Richard Hakluyt became, for all practical purposes, the guardian of his younger cousins. That guardian was a remarkable fellow. A lawyer, he had, as well, an extra-curricular activity: collecting maps, charts, and the written accounts of travellers. To the lawyer this was more than a mere hobby. It was a commercial enterprise. In a day and age when the land masses of the world were imperfectly charted or not charted at all, and very little was known about such faraway lands as India, Java, and the Americas, the sort of data gathered by Hakluyt was invaluable to sea captains and merchants who were planning long voyages.

It was because of his cousin's enthusiasms that the younger Richard Hakluyt became engrossed in the history of English seamanship, and particularly in the voyages of the Elizabethan seamen. According to his own account of it, the tinder of his enthusiasm was ignited during a visit to his cousin when he was 16 and attending Westminster School. He states that during his visit he noticed on his cousin's table "certain books of cosmography, as well as a universal map." The lawyer, quick to sense his young kinsman's interest in the material, gave him a lecture, not only on the geography of the day, but also on the products of little-known and far-off lands, and on what items English merchants should take with them when journeying to those lands.

The lawyer, who had a flair for the dramatic, ended his talk by placing in young Richard's hands the Bible opened to Psalm 107, and directing him to read the 23rd and 24th verses. The boy read: "Some went down to the sea in ships, doing business on the great waters; they saw the deeds of the Lord, His wondrous works in the deep."

For the young Westminster student, it was perhaps the most moving incident in his entire life. He says that he then and there vowed that should he ever be "preferred to the university . . . where better time, and more convenient place might be ministered for these studies, I would by God's assistance prosecute that knowledge and kind of literature. . . ."

He kept that vow when two years later, he was given a studentship to Christchurch College, Oxford. There he remained for seven years while he acquired an M.A. He was ordained a deacon and then a priest in 1578. He was now ready to begin his real life's work. He wasted no time. In 1580 he arranged to have published the accounts of Jacques Cartier's first two voyages to the Americas. These accounts were translations from the Italian versions of the voyages by the historian Giovanni Battista Ramusio. Hakluyt had persuaded John Florio of Oxford to do the translating. Two years later, Hakluyt's own first work appeared: *Divers Voyages.*

That his first work appeared so shortly after his leaving Oxford suggests he must have been gathering material even while he was a student. Probably he was interviewing and getting on paper the narratives of some of Martin Frobisher's men, such as Best, Hall and Settle. Any sailor, merchant prince or between-decks seaman, fascinated him.

Hakluyt himself appears to have travelled no farther than Paris where, from 1582-87, he was chaplain to the English ambassador. Though Hakluyt was to spend a lifetime listening to and recording the exciting tales of others, his Paris sojourn was the only period in which he himself actively took part in what might be termed adventure. At a time when England and Spain were on the verge of war, the embassy in neutral Paris was a hotbed of spies. More than once the still-young clergyman was pressed into service as a courier, conveying, either by diplomatic pouch or by memory, information back to England.

At the same time he continued to pursue his literary ambitions. Within two years after his return to England he published his first version of *The Principall Navigations, Voiages and Discoveries of the English Nation.* Published right after England's victory over the Spanish Armada, the work was regarded as a tribute to England's seamen and probably Hakluyt's final major work.

Fortunately, it proved to be little more than an introduction to his massive version of the same title that appeared in three volumes, the first published in 1598, the last in 1600. No reader who has ever delved seriously into this work would call it anything other than the prose epic of the English people. What his contemporary, Shakespeare, did for English drama, Hakluyt did for English history. For generations Hakluyt's tales were also the only adventure reading young people had. His characters are as vital, as colourful, and as dynamic as those created by Shakespeare—and Hakluyt's characters were real.

Hakluyt himself led an interesting but not adventurous life. In 1587 he married the cousin of Thomas Cavendish, captain of the third ship to circle the world. Her name was Douglasse. She bore him a son and died in 1598. Six years later he remarried, this time to the widow of a London merchant named Smith.

Hakluyt seems to have been on speaking terms with practically every person of importance in the whole of England, including the queen. He went to school with the poet Edmund Spenser. He was acquainted with Shakespeare, who paid Hakluyt a tribute in his play *Twelfth Night* with his mention of "The new map . . . of the Indies." This map was the first really important one ever produced by Englishmen. It is believed Hakluyt worked along with the navigator John Davis on the map. The map was taken from the famous Molineux Globe of 1592. Emeric Molineux, a citizen of Lambeth, is thought to have been selected by Hakluyt to do the actual work, with Hakluyt and Davis both acting as advisors. Hakluyt was no mere dabbler in cartography; indeed, as well as being well known as a writer, he was a renowned geographer. He was acquainted, at least through correspondence, with the Flemish geographer Gerhard Mercator, the father of modern cartography.

Many rewards came to Hakluyt during his lifetime. To aid him in his work, various church appointments, which involved little work but provided him with financial security, were arranged for him through Queen Elizabeth I. The last of these, a post at Westminster Abbey, was bestowed upon him in 1602. He held this post until his death in 1616. Final and lasting tribute was paid him when he was buried in the Abbey.

What a legacy he left us! Realizing he was living in a period of great change, he had the vision to make certain that the events of the period were recorded—not by armchair historians, but by men who had stood, sick and weary, upon the decks of ships thousands of miles from home.

From Hakluyt's enormous works, I have chosen to retell some of the most exciting and most important of the voyages to the Northwest and the South Atlantic, as well as Thomas Cavendish's circumnavigation of the globe and the dramatic voyage of the *Delight* of Bristol. The voyages to the Northwest seem to me to be especially timely in view of the renewed interest in the Arctic. Indeed, interest in the Arctic regions of the world today is as widespread and as keen as the voyages of Master Hore, Martin Frobisher and John Davis are fascinating contrasts to that of Neil Armstrong and the Apollo 11—truly fantastic voyages!

In sixteenth-century England there were no laws for the prevention of cruelty to seamen. That being so, when a certain ship, in 1577, put out from Plymouth with a crew of eighty, every member of her company, from captain to cook's boy, knew very well theirs would not be a pleasure cruise, particularly as the ship expected to be gone for at least two years. During that time her crewmen would have as living quarters the between-decks, a space that, to judge from the tonnage of the ship, could not possibly have exceeded 1,100 square feet—about the floor space of the average bungalow of today. Of course, the entire eighty men would not be jammed into that one tiny area. The half dozen officers would berth above them in the poop; the two or three cooks would probably choose to sleep in the galley or the hold. But even minus those few, the between-decks must have been a sardines-in-a-can arrangement.

At night, or when they were sick, which was often, the men would lie on makeshift beds consisting mainly of odds and ends of worn-out sailcloth or other rags. Their clothing, in most instances, would not be accepted today for anything other than recycling. Besides that, the clothing would be washed only on those rare occasions when the ship touched land. As a result of this, and because the ship's bathing facilities consisted only of a shipmate and a bucket of sea water, the crew would very soon be filthy, smelly and lousy. The toilet was a grating far out on the beak.

Food supplies would appear to have been liberal in quantity, but they consisted, in the main, of items on which no man could hope to remain healthy for long. Here is a typical listing of the weekly rations per man:

Beer	7 gallons
Biscuit or bread	7 pounds
Saltmeat with peas	4 pounds
Saltfish (no size or weight specified)	4⅜ fishes
Butter or olive oil	14 ounces
Cheese	2½ pounds

It is said that the men, who usually ate in fours, made a rule of drawing only two-thirds of their rations; the remaining third they sold back to the ship. Water was never drunk while the beer lasted. The water was usually so bad that any man who drank it must have been dying of thirst.

The facilities for preparing the food were rudimentary. There was a galley, which was located in the bottom of the ship on a bricked floor on top of the ballast. Stoves, as we know them, had yet to be invented. Tudor kitchens ashore had only open spits and bricked ovens—which require chimneys. Pictures of sixteenth-century ships never exhibit anything that can be taken for a chimney. What became of the smoke is a mystery. Nevertheless, poet and sea historian John Masefield claims they did cook in those galleys. It is also known that much of the cooking, weather permitting, was done on the weatherdeck.

Masefield in his introduction to the Everyman's Edition of *Hakluyt's Voyages*, supplies a brief description of life aboard the ships of the period. The ships, he says, were overcrowded, dark, dank, and evil-smelling. The food was terrible. The beer the men were forced to drink, due to the foulness of the water, was prone to cause dysentery. The men themselves were poorly clad, often owning only the rags on their backs, which were usually filthy dirty. Mortality rates from such ailments as scurvy and typhus were appallingly high. He ends his depressing statement by reminding us that, after all, it was the sixteenth century. Plagues, poverty and filth abounded ashore as well as at sea.

The ship used above as an example was Drake's ship, *Golden Hind.* In some ways, however, she was really not typical of her time. Drake, when it came to caring for the comfort of his men, was a century ahead of most captains of his day. He proved this on his epic voyage around the world. It took two years, 10 months and 11 days. Yet the ship returned to Plymouth with 53 or 54 of her original 80 men. This was something of a record. A decade later, the *Delight* of Bristol returned from a much shorter voyage with 6 alive out of a crew of 91. But even Drake had difficulty keeping his men healthy. When he and his men had been 21 months at sea, they captured the Spanish treasure ship, the *Cacafuega.* Later, the Spaniards reported that the Englishmen were in very poor health, with no more than 30 of them well and fit for duty.

Perhaps it was the odds against their coming back from a long voyage—as well as the fact that many of them were press-gang victims—that made sixteenth-century mariners a surly, rebellious lot. Mutinies were common. It may have been to guard against such shows of independence, or merely because the sixteenth century was a cruel age, that shipboard discipline was very strict. The captain of the ship may not have known anything about either ships or navigation, but he had the power of life and death over all men under him. Probably the death penalty was not often invoked. Other penalties, many of them sadistic and cruel, were meted out with considerable frequency. These included floggings and ducking from the yardarm, or being tied to the mast with weights hung from the neck. This latter penalty was said to have been absolute torture. In addition, a man could be put in irons or what was called the bilboes, meaning he could be lashed to the capstan bar, or a grating. What must have been a perfectly horrible punishment was to have a marlinespike, a tool for splicing rope, lashed crosswise into the mouth.

The marlinespike might find its way into a seaman's mouth if he were heard to blaspheme or utter falsehoods. Captains of the sixteenth century, while exhibiting monumental indifference to the earthly comforts of their men, were most circumspect regarding the future of their souls, hence the regulations regarding the sins of blasphemy and lying. And, just in case the seamen might forget there was a God, there were prayers each day and Communion every Sunday.

Golden Hind, even though she was a man-of-war, could have doubled as a merchantman, for merchant ships of the day differed little from the ship-of-war except in guns carried. Fortunately, we know a great deal about *Golden Hind* due to the fact she was long preserved as a sort of national monument. A painting of her is today in the Maritime Museum in Greenwich. From that painting, and reproductions of it, we know she had, besides her long, projecting bowsprit, three masts: fore, main and mizzen. The bowsprit and the mizzen each had a sail; the fore and main had two each, the maincourse and the topsail. She also had what were called bonnets and drabblers—extra canvas which could be attached to the lower edges of the maincourses to increase the spread of sail.

Golden Hind is reported to have been 75 feet from stem to stern, while the length of her maindeck, gundeck, or between-deck, which were all one and the same, is given as 60 feet. Her tonnage was 100 tons. The dimensions supplied us for *Golden Hind* correspond very closely to what is known as the English tonnage rule of 1582. This rule had been devised by a man named Matthew Baker and was based on the number of tons of wine, in hogsheads, a ship could stow. Four hogsheads were reckoned as a ton. Baker also worked out a formula whereby a ship could be built to a reasonably accurate tonnage.

Drake's ship, like all other ships of her day, did not have a wheel. Ship's wheels did not appear until the beginning of the eighteenth century. Her steering apparatus consisted of a rudder and a whipstaffe. The whipstaffe was a great bar which was attached to the rudder and came into the ship through an opening in the stern. Usually located either between-decks or in the mainpoop along with the binnacle, the man, or men, tending it controlled the rudder by moving the whipstaffe back and forth. Ways had been devised whereby blocks could do some of the work. During a severe storm when the ship might be driving (it was called riding ahull) the whipstaffe could be lashed and left untended.

When it came to navigating, the sixteenth-century seaman was hampered most by his lack of an accurate clock or chronometer. Chronometers did not come into general use until the mid-eighteenth century. Before then, pilots had to depend on the sandglass to keep time. Sandglasses can be reasonably accurate if the men tending them are reliable. Watches ended when a certain number of glasses had run. The temptation to flip them before they had completely run was apparently great. A few premature flips and the glass would be out several minutes (four minutes equals a degree of longitude), which probably explains why such a skilled navigator as John Davis could be out as many as 10° when he gave a longitudinal reading. Also it would explain why Hudson Strait appears on old maps as nearly a third longer than it really is.

However when it came to finding his latitude, the seaman of the Elizabethan era had little difficulty. He had two fairly efficient instruments: the astrolabe and the cross-staff. With either of these he could shoot the sun at midday or the North Star at night. If he were south of the Equator he relied on the Southern Cross. Latitudinal readings found in the old accounts are surprisingly accurate.

In the 400 years since these rude methods of navigation and harsh ways of living on shipboard, incredible changes have taken place. Technology has advanced to the point where we send men into space with complicated navigational equipment under conditions which are cramped but otherwise comfortable and humane. What remains the same is the lure and excitement of voyages to unknown places. Because of this, it's not as hard as it seems to go back in time in imagination to the ships that put out from Plymouth with Frobisher or Davis or Cavendish.

ACCORDING TO *Hakluyt*

PART ONE

Voyages to the Northwest

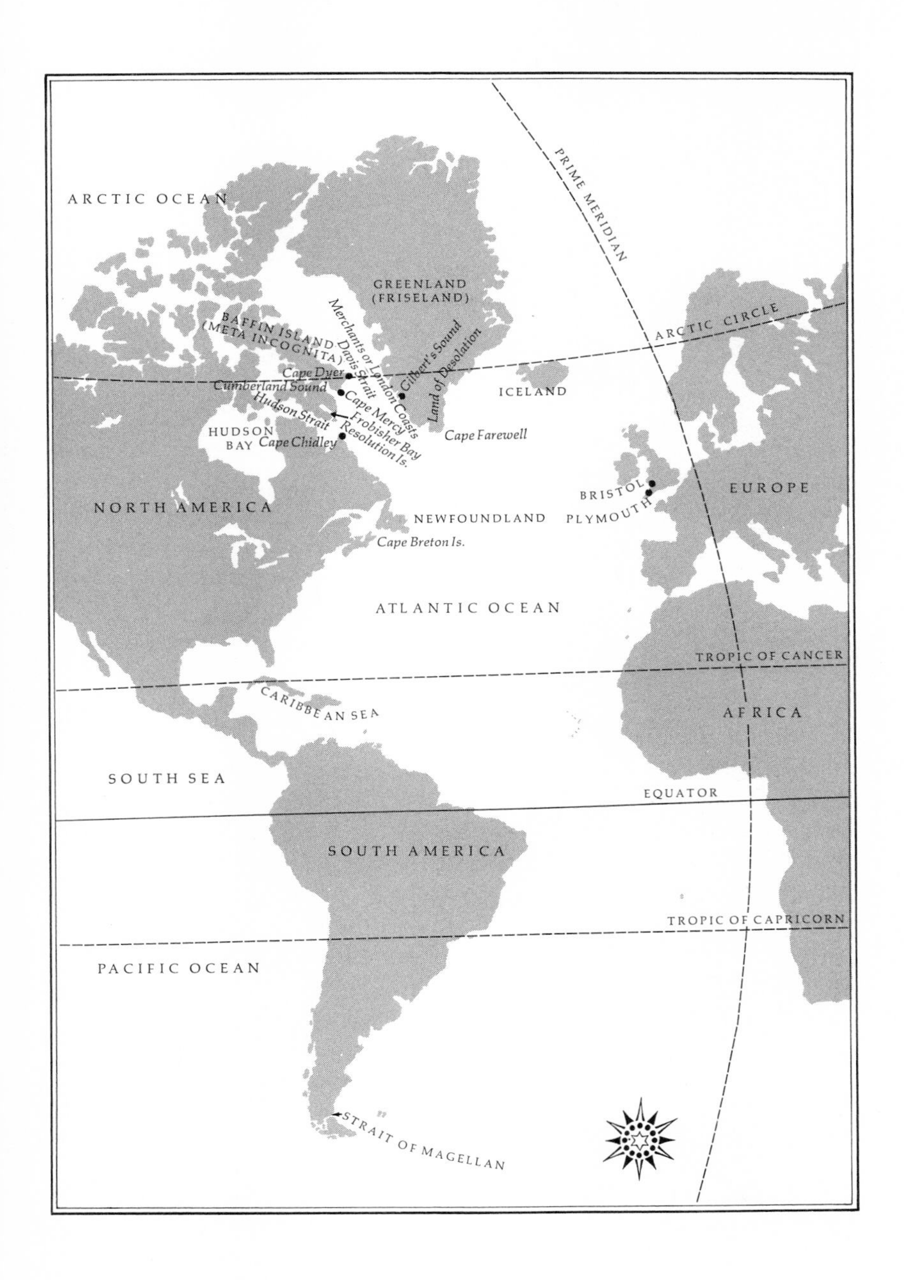
ARCTIC OCEAN
PRIME MERIDIAN
GREENLAND
(FRISELAND)
BAFFIN ISLAND
(META INCOGNITA)
Merchants or London Coasts
Davis Strait
Gilbert's Sound
Land of Desolation
ARCTIC CIRCLE
Cape Dyer
Cumberland Sound
Cape Mercy
Hudson Strait
Frobisher Bay
Resolution Is.
HUDSON
BAY
Cape Chidley
ICELAND
Cape Farewell
BRISTOL
PLYMOUTH
EUROPE
NORTH AMERICA
NEWFOUNDLAND
Cape Breton Is.
ATLANTIC OCEAN
TROPIC OF CANCER
CARIBBEAN SEA
AFRICA
SOUTH SEA
EQUATOR
SOUTH AMERICA
TROPIC OF CAPRICORN
PACIFIC OCEAN
STRAIT OF MAGELLAN

The voyage of

Master Hore

as told by Masters Dawbeny and Buts

Master Hore cannot be referred to as either a great sea captain or an explorer. The term blundering amateur fits him better. The account of his voyage is given here for two reasons: Hore and his company exemplify the spirit of adventure that permeated sixteenth-century England; and the story tells us a great deal about the Hakluyts, particularly the younger Richard who, upon learning, many years after the voyage, that a member of Master Hore's company was still alive, immediately mounted his horse and rode, he says, 200 miles in order that he might, "Learne the whole trueth of this voyage from his own mouth."

Master Hore of London, a man of goodly stature, great courage, and much given to the study of cosmography, did, in the year 1536, encourage divers gentlemen, as well as others, to accompany him on a voyage of discovery to the northwest parts of America, namely Cape Breton and Newfoundland. As King Henry VIII who was then in the twenty-eighth year of his reign favoured such a voyage, Master Hore's persuasiveness soon had many gentlemen, including a Master Buts, coming forward and willingly entering into the action with him. It is from Master Buts' mouth I wrote most of this relation.

Master Buts accompanied Master Hore in the *Trinity*, a goodly ship of seven score [140] tons burden. There was besides the *Trinity*, a second ship named the *Minion*. The whole number that went into the two ships totalled six score persons, thirty of these being gentlemen. All mustered at Gravesend and, after receiving the Sacrament, embarked from there at the end of April.

From their date of departure from Gravesend, more than two months passed without their either sighting or touching land. Then they came to a part of the West Indies they believed to be Cape Breton. From there, they shaped their course northeastwards until they came to the Island of Penguin. This island is full of rocks and stones but upon it nest many great fowls, which in colour are white and grey, and in size somewhat like geese. Many of these fowls, which cannot fly, were driven into the boats. Later they were flayed, to save the labour of plucking, and their meat was found to be both good and nourishing. In that place, too, bears, both black and white, were seen. Some of the bears were also killed for their meat.

Master Oliver Dawbeny, who was in the *Minion,* told Master Richard Hakluyt the following: Having left the Island of Penguin, and arriving in a harbour in Newfoundland, the ships lay at anchor for several days, during which time there were no signs of the people of the country. Then one day Master Dawbeny was alone on deck when he spied a boat with savages in it, which boat was coming down the bay toward the ships. He at once called to those who were beneath the hatches to come up if they wished to see the people. The entire company came up, and upon seeing that the savages were still rowing toward the ships, a number of gentlemen and seamen quickly lowered and manned the ship's boat. They put off, with the intention of meeting the savages and capturing them. But the savages, guessing what our men had in mind, turned and fled to an island up the bay.

Our men pursued them onto the island, but the savages once more fled, this time leaving behind them some of their belongings, including a side of bear meat which was roasting, on a wooden spit, over a fire. Nearby was found a boot made from leather, the calf of which was decorated with a handiwork of fine lines. Too, a warm mitten lay close to the boot. Taking those items with them, our men returned to the ship and reported to us they had seen nothing else on the island except soil and trees, the trees being both fir and pine.

Master Dawbeny further said that while the ships continued to lie at anchor, the company ran so short on victuals men took to watching the nest of an osprey, and to robbing it of the fishes the mother osprey hourly brought to her young. The famine increasing still further, they were forced to subsist on what roots and herbs they could find on the land, but alas, these poor items did not satisfy their great hunger. Then one day two men went into the forest to hunt for roots and while one was stooping, and so had his back turned, his mate slew him! That same mate cut off pieces of his flesh and broiled them over a fire before devouring them.

Other men did the same, murdering so they could eat, and the company decreased in number with the officers believing the missing men had either been eaten by wild beasts or slain by the savages. This continued until one day a member of the company, driven by his hunger, went alone into the forest in search of whatever he might find by way of food. While about his task, there came to him the odour of flesh being broiled. Soon thereafter he came upon the person who was cooking the meat. In great anger, he reviled the man for enjoying plenty while his fellows starved. So cruel were his speeches, the owner of the meat could contain himself no longer but burst out with these words, "If you wouldst know, the meat you see cooking came from the buttocks of a man!"

The report of this having been brought back to the ship, the captain forthwith mustered the company and made a notable oration. Such dealings, he said, could not but offend the Almighty, and then he quoted from the Scriptures, giving instances where God, when called upon, had come to the assistance of those in distress. The power of the Almighty, he told them, was no less then than it had ever been. He then added that if it had not pleased God to aid them in their present distress, it would be better to perish in body, and live everlasting, than to relieve for a short time their mortal bodies but be condemned, later, to the everlasting fires of hell. He ended by advising all of the company to repent and pray, in the hope God would hear and, having heard, would relieve them.

The famine, though, increased rather than lessened, whereupon the men, fearful that all would perish, agreed among themselves to cast lots to see who should be killed. But such was the mercy of God that that same night there arrived in port a French ship that was well victualled. The English quickly made themselves masters of it, and victualling one of their own and changing the other for the French ship, they set sail for England.

In their journey homeward they sailed so far to the northward they saw mighty islands of ice upon which hawks and other fowls, weary from flying, were resting. They also saw certain great white fowls with red beaks and legs, which were somewhat larger than herons and judged them to be some sort of stork. They arrived at St. Ives in Cornwall about the end of October.

Master Buts, from hunger and misery, was so changed in appearance his father, Sir William, and his mother, Lady Buts, refused to believe he was their son until he showed them a wart, a wart only they knew about, growing upon his knee. This Master Buts told me, Richard Hakluyt of Oxford, when I had ridden 200 miles so as to learn the whole truth of this voyage from his own mouth, he being the only man now alive that was on the voyage.

Months after their arrival in England, the Frenchmen also came to England, and made complaints directly to King Henry. The king caused the matter to be gone into thoroughly, and upon finding that the great distress of his subjects had caused them to deal in such a manner with the French, he was moved to pity and gave orders that none should be punished. Out of his own royal purse he recompensed the French.

The first voyage of

Martin Frobisher

as told by George Best

Martin Frobisher was born circa 1540 in Yorkshire of Welsh ancestry. At the age of fourteen he was already at sea—on a voyage to the coast of Guinea in West Africa. There is no record of how old Frobisher was when he took command of his first ship; however, as he was called upon to answer charges of piracy allegedly committed by him off the coast of Africa in 1566, obviously he was in command by that date.

At about that same time, Frobisher began to take a keen interest in stories suggesting that a northwest passage around the north of America to the Orient might exist. Such a passage would provide English merchants and traders with a much shorter, cheaper and more direct route to Cathay, as China was then called, and all of its riches than the existing overland route or the long sea route around Africa and India. Finally, after fifteen years, Frobisher succeeded in convincing a wealthy patron, the Earl of Warwick, to back a voyage.

George Best, who wrote this account of the journey, described himself as "a gentleman employed on the same voyage." Master Best was obviously a first-rate seaman. Certainly Frobisher had confidence in him, for on his second voyage to the northwest, Best is listed as lieutenant to Frobisher himself, and on the third voyage he was captain of the *Anne Francis*.

Frobisher prepared two small barks, the *Gabriel* and the *Michael*, each of twenty-five tons burden, and a pinnace of ten tons, and had all three of them victualled for a full twelve months. With them, he departed from Blackwall 15 June, 1576.

Sailing on a northwesterly course from England until 11 July, he sighted a high and ragged land which he judged must be Friseland [Greenland], but he dared not venture too near this land by reason of a great icefield. It happened too, he was hindered by fogs and mists. It was while off Friseland that a most violent storm descended upon them. Its fury was such the pinnace with its crew of four was driven to the bottom and the *Michael* also vanished. However, the *Michael* was not sunk. Instead, her company, finding themselves unable to reunite with the general's ship, and deeming it sunk like the pinnace, returned to England with that report.

Captain Frobisher, nothwithstanding these misfortunes, and regardless also of damage to his own ship, which had had her mainmast sprung and her topmast completely blown away, continued the voyage and held a course to the northwest so that on 20 July he sighted a high land. He called it Queen Elizabeth Foreland [Resolution Island]. Changing course then and sailing in a more northerly direction, he soon raised another foreland. Between these two forelands there lies a great bay, gut, or passage dividing the mainlands or continents. There he met with quantities of ice, and contrary winds, and so was thwarted from continuing into the strait he had discovered. However, within a few days more favourable winds, aided by currents, scattered the ice and he proceeded with the avowed purpose of finding how long the strait was and if it opened, as was his hope, into a sea. He passed into the strait for all of fifty leagues and still had land on either side. The land on his right hand he judged to be the continent of Asia; that on his left the mainland of America. Recalling that Magellan had given his own name to a strait, our general called the one he had found Frobisher's Strait.

When he had taken his ship another ten leagues into his strait, he went ashore and found where fires had been laid. He also saw a mighty deer which, without warning, charged him and forced him to flee for his life. That danger past, he ventured to the top of a high hill and from there perceived several objects out to sea. At first, he believed these to be either whales or other sea animals; but upon their coming closer in he saw them to be boats of leather [kayaks]. It was while both his thoughts and his eyes were occupied with the strange boats that he became aware that some of the people of the country were lurking among the nearby rocks. Their intent was, at least in his opinion, to get between him and the ship's boat which had brought him ashore. He descended the hill in the greatest of haste so as to get aboard.

Afterward, he made sundry contacts with these people so that various of them ventured aboard the ship, bringing with them gifts of salmon and the raw flesh of animals. They were persuaded to exchange the skins of seals and white bears for trinkets such as bells and beads made from glass. They also, in great good humour, demonstrated they could climb the rigging as well, and even better, than the nimblest of the seamen. In this manner they gained the confidence of the mariners who, despite the warning of their captain, trusted them fully.

This led to misadventure. Five of our men took the ship's boat and went ashore to exchange gifts with the people. They were taken prisoner and have not been heard from since. Their capture was unfortunate, for, not only were we now without a ship's boat, but the loss of five seamen left us with scarcely sufficient men to sail the bark back home. Any hope we might recover our lost mariners was thwarted by the people. Knowing well they had done wrong, they became wary and would no longer come aboard the ship or even near to it.

It was then our captain vowed he would deceive the deceivers. Knowing well they delighted in our toys and trinkets, and especially in bells, he got a bell and rang it continuously. When the people approached, in their boats, close enough to listen, the captain made signs they could have the bell. But they remained wary and kept well away from the ship's side. Our captain was undaunted. He flung them a bell, purposely pretending he could not throw it far enough so that it fell into the sea and was lost. Then to make them more greedy, he got and began ringing a bell which was both larger and louder. This one, though, he would not throw. Instead, he made signs that any man could have it who would approach close enough to the ship's side to take it from his hand. One of the people thought to do this. But when he reached to take the bell, the captain grasped him by the hand and, with a mighty heave, hauled both the man and his boat aboard. The native's anger was so great that in his ensuing struggles to escape he bit his tongue in twain. However, of the wound to his tongue he did not die; he lived until we reached England but then died from a cold he had contracted from the seamen while still at sea.

This captive Captain Frobisher regarded as sufficient proof to take home with him that we had been to distant lands inhabited by infidels whose like had never before been seen. We departed and arrived in England, at Harwich, on 2 October, where Captain Frobisher was highly commended, more particularly as he brought hope of a passage to Cathay.

The voyage was thus ended, but more can be said of it. It is to be remembered that upon our first arriving in Frobisher's Strait, there were such vast quantities of ice in the sea we were thwarted in attempts to get ashore. Divers attempts were made before a boat managed to land. When one did, our captain charged its crew members to bring items of the country back aboard with them. In carrying out his order, some of the men brought grasses; others flowers. One returned with a piece of black stone, much like a sea cabbage [a brown alga] in colour, while its weight led many to believe it must be some sort of metal or mineral. This piece of ore our captain regarded as of no value, though he kept it by him as a novelty. Upon his arrival in London, sundry of his friends besieged him with requests for things which he might have brought back with him from the strange land. He had little to give them, other than bits broken from the piece of black stone.

As it fortuned, a gentlewoman, one who was also the wife of one of the adventurers who had accompanied the captain, either by design or mischance, threw her piece of rock into the fire. It remained there a good long time. Upon its owner removing it and attempting to cleanse it with vinegar, particles of it glistened not unlike gold. It aroused great interest; it was taken to goldfiners who pronounced it rich in gold. These same goldfiners were anxious to know if there was much of the ore where that particular piece had been found. Upon being assured there was considerable quantity of it, they immediately presented themselves to Captain Frobisher and offered to go with him in search of it.

In conclusion, such hope was kindled that many men of means came forward with offers of money in order that a further voyage might be attempted.

The ore which had been pronounced gold was later discovered to be iron pyrites, more commonly called fool's gold.

The mighty deer which ran at Frobisher was likely an old muskox bull, who had lost his harem to a younger male. Such frustrated animals wander alone and sour-natured, and have been known to attack men.

The five missing seamen Frobisher claimed had been taken prisoner by the Eskimos had probably deserted. This theory is borne out by information an American, Charles Hall, came upon while wintering in the vicinity of Frobisher Bay during the years 1860-61. Not only did Hall find relics of Frobisher's expedition, but the local Eskimos could still repeat the story of the missing seamen. Prisoners they may have been to begin with—but not always. The Eskimos accepted them, and for four years they lived with the natives. Then they built a boat from materials left behind by Frobisher on his third voyage. Although the Eskimos tried to dissuade them, they sailed away and that is the last ever heard of them.

The second voyage of

Martin Frobisher

as told by Dionese Settle

On Whitsunday, 26 May 1577, Captain Frobisher departed Blackwall in three of the Queen Majesty's ships: the *Aide* of 180 tons, and the barks *Gabriel* and *Michael*, the *Gabriel* being captained by Master Fenton, a gentleman of my Lord of Warwick's, and the *Michael* by Master York, a gentleman of my Lord Admiral's. One hundred and forty persons, gentlemen, soldiers and sailors comprised the company; the venture was well-victualled for one-half year. Our general's stated purpose on this, his second voyage, was for the further discovering of a shorter route to Cathay, as well as for the better exploration of lands found by him the year previous.

Stopping at Harwich for a final checking on our ships and supplies, and finding both as they should be, we then hoisted our sails and proceeded northward with such a merry wind that we fell in with the Orkneys on 7 June. At that place our general thought it opportune we take on a further supply of fresh water so, accordingly, he sent boats and men ashore. However, the people, upon seeing our men, fled before them in great alarm and it was, therefore, with the greatest difficulty contact was made with them in order that they might be assured no harm was intended them. They live, it seems, in constant dread of pirates who are wont to swoop down and rob them of what little they possess. The lives of these people are rude and simple. The islands being destitute of wood, their houses, which they share with their cattle, are built of stone and lack chimneys. For warmth, turf and dried dung are burned. The smoke thus created escapes through an opening in the centre of the roof. A Christian people, they farm and fish, taking great quantities of the latter which are dried in the sun and used, not alone for food, but as items of trade.

We departed from there on 8 June and held our course to the west and northwest. After six days of sailing we began to meet with floating evergreen trees, which trees were borne on a current flowing from west to east, leading us to believe the trees came from the new found land. On 4 July we came within sight of Friseland, finding it surrounded by icefields which stretched out as many as ten or even twelve leagues from the shore. Here also we sighted great icebergs which showed above the water, in some instances, for as many as forty fathoms [240 feet]. Supposing them to be aground due their size, we took soundings but scarce could find bottom with our lead. It was in this region also that we tasted the most boisterous of boreal [Arctic] blasts, winds which came mixed with hail and snow so that it was equal to our own winter, despite its being the month of July and the latitude not above 61°.

Our captain on three different days took the ship's boat and with it attempted to get ashore but on each occasion he was thwarted by the bulwark of ice. We could discern though, that the coast of Friseland is fringed with very high mountains which are completely covered with snow, except in such places as their very steepness prohibits this. It appears also to be a coast much subject to dense fogs. For four days we worked our way along the southern edge of the icefield, without seeing a single sign of human habitation. However, flocks of small birds came from the land and flew about the ships, causing us to suppose that the country inland might be more habitable.

Leaving there on 8 July, we again raised land on 16 July, which land was the same our general had found the year previous and named the Queen's Foreland [on Resolution Island]. It is an island lying close to the continent of America; opposite it and northward of it lies another island and it is called Halles Island after the master of the ship. This isle lies close against the mainland of what our general believes to be the continent of America. Between these two islands is the entrance, a wide one, to Frobisher's Strait, which strait is supposed to give passage into the Sea of Sur [South Sea].

The strait we found shut up with ice. However, our general was undaunted and had two pinnaces prepared and manned, and with them passed into the strait by working amid the ice. Before leaving, and in order to assure they might not come to harm, he ordered the ships to stay well out and not to venture into the ice. While our general was examining the eastern shore of the strait, a number of the people of the country appeared and acted in a most strange manner, namely leaping and dancing while at the same time they uttered loud shrieks. Our general sought to make contact with them by landing and leaving presents of knives and other items on the shore, after which he and his party withdrew to a distance. The natives came and took the proffered gifts and, after leaving some items of their own, departed a way.

Finally, two of them were emboldened to leave their weapons and come forward. Our general and the master went forward to meet them, after charging the remainder of the company to remain back. After certain friendly signs had been exchanged between the people and our general, members of the company came forward and sought to lay hands on them. They became greatly alarmed and one broke free and escaped. He ran to his fellow countrymen who, in anger, began to shoot arrows at the company. But our own archers, being well prepared for such a happening, shot arrows of their own. Various of the people were hurt and all of them fled.

While the general and his company continued to busy themselves searching the eastern shore of the strait, as well as the islands adjacent to it, the ships continued to lie offshore though they dared not put too far out as the boats had scant store of victuals aboard. By this action they were endangered as they were caught by night in a tempest.

Ice came thick about the ships, some of it in such monstrous pieces that even the least of them could have shivered a ship into portions. This they would indeed have done to all of our ships had not God (He at all times watches over man in his infirmities) provided light whereby we could avoid the most imminent of the dangers. Fourteen times during one four-hour watch we were forced to take measures to avoid injuries to our ships. But by the valour of our master gunner, as well as that of the two master's mates, namely Masters Jackman and Dier, all of them expert in navigation, we continued to hold the ships close to the mouth of the strait, thus putting the safety of the general and his company before our own.

The following day, 19 July, our general and his men returned to us, bringing with them great tidings. They had found what they believed to be vast riches in the rocks of the mountains. We had still more cause for cheer that day, for the winds which had threatened us with destruction had also worked to our good by dispersing the ice and driving it out to sea and by doing so had cleared the strait. That being so, our general, who during his absence from us had discovered a fair harbour on the western shore, ordered the ships to proceed to that harbour, which we did. All of the company were at that time in good health and spirits, except for one man. He, by God's will, had died.

When the ships were in and riding safely at anchor, our general had the entire company kneel so that we might give proper thanks to God for our safe arrival. On that occasion also he pleaded with God to bless our Queen, for whom he was claiming all of the lands he had found or would find; last, he beseeched His Divine Majesty to make it possible for us to, through Christian effort, save the people of the country from paganism and bring them to a knowledge of the true religion, and to the hope of salvation in Christ the Redeemer. Those things in order, our general addressed us further, charging all of us to be obedient to our officers, mentioning in particular Masters Fenton and York and his personal lieutenant, Master Beast [Best]. These officers, he said, would remain with the ships while he, and a goodly number of men, would be absent on a journey into the land.

Shortly thereafter we marched inland, in good order, with flags displayed and weapons ready, this last in case there should be trouble from the people of the country. Our main intention during this march was to erect mounds of stone and do various other things, all for the purpose of informing the subjects of foreign princes that the country had already been claimed for our Queen.

During our absence those who remained aboard stood constant watch as the ships were in constant danger from the ice, great quantities of which came into the harbour with each tide. They fended it off by various means, and on occasion even towed pieces of it away by boat. As a result of this, fair warning can be issued to all who would navigate these seas that the threats are many and include, not alone the ice just mentioned, but extreme winds and furious seas. Finally, our general returned, having searched the land sufficiently to ascertain it contained no great riches. Straightway, he took the two barks and crossed over to the eastern shore, hoping to land and find much richness thereof, a natural thought as the stones of this place glister [glisten] in the sun, as do some of the sands as well, yet this quality in them only verifies the old proverb: All is not gold that glistereth.

Following the departure of the barks, those of us remaining in the ship found a dead fish floating in the sea. It was a strange creature with a great horn from out its nose, which horn we measured and found it to be only two inches less than six feet. It was also hollow. This last we perceived as its tip was broken off. Some of the seamen, though this I did not witness, caught some spiders and placed them within the hollow of the horn: The spiders died very shortly, whereupon we supposed the beast to be a sea unicorn.

Meanwhile, our general having located a good harbour, as well as huge stores of the supposed gold ore, returned aboard the *Michael*. With the *Michael,* he proceeded to do some further exploring of the strait, and in so doing they spied, on the western side and not too distant from the ship, two tents of sealskin. Accompanied by a number of men he approached these tents but the inhabitants fled. Nevertheless, he and his men entered the tents and left various trifles such as glass beads, bells, and knives, taking in return a large dog. They left, as well, pen, paper and ink and a written message for the five men, in the event they were still alive, who had been taken captive by the natives the previous voyage. Our general was most determined to ascertain the fate of his missing men. To that end, and on the same day, he had all the men ashore that it was safe to take out of the ships. He charged us to make contact, by any means possible, with the people.

Upon our coming to where the tents had been, we found they had been removed and set up farther along the shore and close to the water, from which we judged it was in the minds of the people that if we bothered them further they could escape by boat. Hoping to outwit them, we divided ourselves into two companies, one staying in the pinnaces, the other landing and rounding a mountain so as to come upon them by surprise. When we came upon them, they did not tarry but fled to their boats, leaving the most of their oars behind them so great was their haste. This worked to our advantage for, as they rowed down the bay, our pinnaces met them and had no difficulty in driving them ashore.

When they had landed they defended themselves by shooting their arrows, but our men returned arrows of their own so that three of the natives were wounded. At that, most of the natives escaped by fleeing up the steep rocks. But not all escaped thus. The three wounded men as well as two women and a small child remained behind. The wounded men, rather than accept capture, leaped off the rocks into the sea and were drowned; the women and the child we took. The older of the women, whom various of the seamen suspected of being a witch she was so ugly, had her footwear torn off in order that the men might ascertain whether or not she was cloven-hooved. Finding her feet to be as their own, she was allowed to go free. The younger woman, who was quite comely, was kept, as was her child. The place where this occurred we named Bloody Point, while the harbour was called York's Sound after Master York of the *Michael.*

Having by now a knowledge of the fierceness of the people, and knowing well they would never come unto us in friendship, we became more cruel than was our wont. Entering their tents we took anything which suited our fancy. In those same tents we found a shirt, a doublet and a girdle, as well as some shoes, all of which belonged to the men lost the year before.

On 3 August, we returned to the ship which had by then lain at anchor in the same harbour for thirteen days. Our general had given orders that she be moved across the strait to the harbour where the barks lay, and this was done. He had also made known to us that he wished all three ships to be freighted with enough of the supposed gold ore as he judged would pay, not only the expenses of the first voyage to the region, but the second one as well.

As we were setting about this task, some of the people of the country showed themselves to us on the main shore. This prompted our general, who still desired news of his missing seamen, to once again attempt to come to friendly terms with them. Accordingly, in the ship's boat and with a few men he drew near to the people and made signs indicating he meant them no harm. These tokens, or signs, having been returned by the people, our general at once inquired again about his missing men. The people signified that three of the five were still alive. They then requested we give them pen and ink and paper, which articles they would take to the missing men. They, further, or so nearly as we could judge, promised to show themselves at the selfsame spot four days hence, bringing their prisoners with them.

As proof they still did not trust us fully, they would not take the writing materials from our hands; instead, we had to place the items on the beach and depart well out to sea before they would venture to lay hands upon them. However, on the fourth day and as they had promised, they once again showed themselves on the shore. This pleased our general greatly, for he was certain his men would either be returned to him or, at very least, he would receive messages from them. He, therefore, took a boat and a sufficient number of men and went to where the natives were. On this occasion they showed such great signs of friendship, and in all ways appeared so eager that our general and his men land and visit with them, that some of the seamen, as well as the general himself, became suspicious it might be a trap. This was confirmed when some of the company perceived that men with weapons were lurking amid the rocks farther back. At that, the general refused to have further dealings with them and returned to the ship.

On another day, while the general was examining the coastline from a pinnace, three of the crafty villains appeared at the water's edge holding aloft and waving a white skin. Once again our general, hoping he might receive tiding from his lost men, ordered the boat in close. But once again our seamen perceived that armed men were concealing themselves among the rocks. Failing to lure either the general or any of his company onto the land, they then placed meat upon the beach and departed. This meat we took aboard by means of a boathook, vowing to serve it to our prisoners who, until then, had not been able to digest the food given them.

Seeing we had accepted their offering, they made yet a further attempt to lure the general and his men ashore. They carried a seeming cripple, one who appeared to have no use of his limbs and was also without weapons, down to the shore and, having seated him on a rock, departed. They hoped, no doubt, that our company would not fear an unarmed and impotent man, and hence would be tempted into landing in order to converse with him. However, our general, fully aware it might be a device, sought to test and even possibly cure the supposed cripple. He ordered a soldier to fire his caliver [a hand gun] so that the bullet would pass close to the man's face. This was done, whereupon the cripple leaped to his feet and ran away with great swiftness. At that his companions, many of whom had been hiding among the rocks, began to shoot arrows at us. In return and in order that they might hereafter stand in more fear of us, several calivers were shot at them. Some were hurt and all of them fled.

In attempting to decipher the intent behind all their stratagems, we concluded they were desirous of taking some of us prisoner, so that we might be exchanged for those of their people which we held.

From those prisoners of ours, which we treated with kindness and had learned to converse with by signs, we learned much about the people of the country and their ways. In body, though this we knew from our own observations, they are of good proportions with skins not much darker than our own when it has been burned by the sun. They wear their hair long, the women braiding theirs into two loops. The clothing of the women differs little from that of the men, all of it being made from the skins of such beasts as they can take. For this purpose also the skins and the feathers of fowls are employed. Though they cook much of their food, they are not averse to eating it raw. Their dwellings vary in nature; in summer they may be entirely of skins or have stone walls and skin roofs. As they would be unable to endure the cold winter in such structures, we conjectured they must have their winter abodes elsewhere!

Their weapons are bows and arrows, darts and slings. The bows are of wood, backed by sinews and a yard in length; the arrows for them are half that long. The heads of their arrows and darts are made, in the main, from bone, though some are of iron, these leading us to believe they must have conversation with other people and through exchange obtain the metal. Their boats are of two sorts. One is large and long and able to accommodate as many as a score, while the other is made for a single man who rows with one oar. Both are made from skins sewn over frames of wood.

They own certain large dogs not unlike wolves which they yoke together, as we do oxen, to sleds and by this means transport their belongings from place to place. These same dogs, and this our captives by perfect signs made clear to us, are eaten during times of food scarcity.

What knowledge these people have of God, or indeed what idols they adore, we never learned. We conjectured, though, that they might very well be cannibals, for there is no flesh or fish which they find dead, no matter how filthily it smells, which they will not devour. No doubt necessity forces such practices upon them, for the land is barren except for mosses and some grasses; however, there are great numbers of deer whose heads are adorned by horns which are greater by far than those of any deer found here in this country. Too, the feet of these same deer are marvellously large, measuring as many as seven inches in breadth. There are also hares, wolves, sea bears, and sea fowls of sundry sorts.

On 24 August, having by then taken aboard our vessels sufficient of the supposed gold ore as was deemed advisable for their safety, we departed. The 17 September we fell in with Land's End and from there came to harbour in Milford Haven in Wales. We were alone, having become separated from the barks which had vanished during a three-day tempest. Howbeit, God restored both with one coming safely into Bristol, the other into Yarmouth. In this voyage we lost two men, one by way of God's visitation; the other cast overboard during the tempest.

The third voyage of

Martin Frobisher

as told by George Best

The general, upon returning from his second voyage, repaired with haste to Windsor, where the Court was, so that he might, in person, inform Her Majesty of the success of the voyage and to acquaint her fully with the abundance of gold ore which he had brought back. He was courteously received by Her Majesty who, upon learning the gold ore held promise of great riches and, too, that there was still hope a passage to Cathay would be found, immediately appointed commissioners to look well into the entire affair. She also, upon that same occasion, named the land which had been discovered, Meta Incognita, a most proper name for it insofar as it had, until then, been utterly unknown.

The commissioners went about their tasks without delay; trial was made of the ore; the possibility of a passage to Cathay being found, and the profits which would accrue from such a discovery were also fully examined. Their deliberations concluded, they informed Her Majesty that a third voyage was worthy of being undertaken, and that preparations for the voyage should begin immediately. The commissioners further advised that, as the production from the mines already discovered would more than balance the expenses of the proposed venture, to say naught of the promise those same mines held for the future, a certain number of men should remain to winter in the land. To that end, a strong fort, or house, should be so framed and devised that it could be taken apart and re-erected at will. The proposed building could be transported in parts to Meta Incognita in the holds of ships.

When word of the great adventure got about, a large number of young gentlemen came forward, begging to be among those who would abide the year round in the new land. It was arranged that Captain Fenton, lieutenant to the general, would be given the honour of commanding the men who would inhabit the land, and with him would be Captains Best and Philpot. The whole number of men under them would be one hundred. Of that hundred, forty would be mariners, thirty would be miners, and the remainder would consist of gentlemen, soldiers, goldfiners, bakers, carpenters, and other necessary persons.

The spring following, and when all was in readiness, our general had fifteen goodly ships, all of them well manned and victualled, under his command. Before setting sail he and all of his captains repaired to Greenwich, where the Court was lying, in order to take proper leave of Her Majesty the Queen. Her Majesty received them graciously and, as a mark of her esteem, bestowed upon the general a chain of gold. That ceremony over, the general, and each of his captains, kissed Her Majesty's hand and departed from her presence, going at once to their ships. Thus it was that on 31 May 1578, the fleet departed Harwich and set course for Meta Incognita.

On 6 June while off Cape Clear in Ireland, we sighted what we believed to a pirate ship and gave chase to it. However, on our coming up with it, we learned it had aboard only a company of poor men from Bristol who, a few days previous, had themselves been the victims of pirates. A French rover had stripped their ship clean of all goods and victuals, leaving them in sorry condition as some had been slain and others wounded in the action. Upon seeing their woeful plight, our general was moved. He had our chirurgeons [surgeons] relieve their pains as best they could; he then gave them such supplies and necessities as would see them safely to port.

This good deed done, we held to our appointed course, seeing naught for a fortnight except the sea and a few fowls, namely wilmots, noddies, and gulls. But on 20 June at two of the clock in the morning, and still daylight, we saw what we judged must be a part of Friseland. Here, Captain Frobisher and certain other gentlemen took the ship's boat and, despite much drift ice, managed to get ashore. By so doing, they became, so far as is known, the first Christians ever to set foot on that land. Our general formally took possession of it in the name of Her Majesty. Too, he renamed it West England.

While they were ashore, they came upon several tents, or skin dwellings, belonging to the people of the country, and would willingly have conversed with the owners had not these owners, upon seeing the captain and his companions, fled in terror. Their unguarded tents were entered and searched, with result many strange and interesting items were revealed, including some well-formed boards of firwood and a box of small iron nails. The last, in particular, caused much discussion, with our men finally concluding the people must, at some time, have had trade with civilized countries. Our general was strict in forbidding his men to take anything away with them. However, two large dogs were brought off. But payment in the form of bells, looking glasses, and trinkets was left.

On 23 June, favoured with a fair and strong wind, we left West England astern and set our course for Frobisher's Strait. However, we were soon forced to sail in a more southerly direction because of the great masses of drift ice we encountered. Thick [foggy] weather and mists also caused us trouble. Other dangers threatened. On 30 June we found ourselves in the midst of an immense number of great whales, and one of our ships, the *Salamander*, had the bad fortune to strike one of the monsters while under full courses of sail and with bonnets as well. For a time the ship was halted and stood still. Then the whale made a great and ugly noise and dove. Two days from then we came upon the body of a whale floating in the sea. We wondered if it were not the same one.

On 2 July we raised Queen's Foreland and bore up to it through thick ice; by evening, though with difficulty, we had entered some distance into the strait. Further passage was denied us as of then as the strait was choked, from one side to the other, with mountains of ice. The ice was, this year, more of a cumbrance in every respect than on the previous ones, perhaps by reason of the easterly and southerly winds which kept it from drifting, or being carried by the tides, out to sea. Refusing to be daunted, we tried working our way forward; one ship would find an opening, no matter how narrow, in the ice. It would enter and the other ships would try following its lead. In attempting this, the ships were in constant danger, for even though they followed hard on each other, the ice still contrived to close and shut off passage between them. It is simple truth there was not a ship which did not, and more than once, strike hard. However, as best we could, we proceeded slowly forward, but in so doing the ships became more and more separated. The *Judith,* in which was the lieutenant general, Captain Fenton, disappeared and was believed by many to be lost. The *Michael* also vanished and we knew not her fate.

Then before our very eyes a terrible thing occurred! We lost the *Dennis.* That unfortunate ship, while endeavouring to pass between two mountains of ice, struck one of them such a blow her timbers were stove and she began to take water heavily. Her master, seeing she was doomed, immediately had her gunner shoot off their greatest piece of ordnance. Boats from other ships responded so quickly, and valiantly, that all of the *Dennis'* seamen were saved.

More costly than the loss of the *Dennis* herself: In her hold she had carried numerous parts of the house-to-be! As of then, though, we could devote no time to worrying about the house. Right after the *Dennis* went to the bottom, our perils multiplied when a tempest came raging at us from out of the southwest, the worst direction as it brought still more ice about us from the sea. Greatly distressed, we could go neither forward nor back, and were forced into using every device thinkable in the hope we could save our ships and our very lives. We slung cables, beds, spars, planks and boards which had been intended for our fort, indeed anything we deemed might help, over the sides to act as fenders. Men lined the rails, by day and by night, and with poles, pikes, oars, or just pieces of timber exerted all of their strength in desperate efforts to ward off the ice. At times when the peril was greatest, men even went down onto the ice itself and, while standing on it, put their shoulders to the ship's side and pushed mightily, hoping thereby to ease the pressure on the timbers. Amid these extremes, and as we strove to save what was mortal of us, we did not neglect to pray to the Almighty, for we knew that in Him lay our final hope, both in this world and the next.

After a night and a day of this it pleased the Almighty to reverse the wind so that it came at us from the west-northwest. When that happened, the ice in the strait was driven out to sea, and we were allowed to escape to more open water. Alas, though, we could not rest; we had to fall at once to work mending timbers, masts, sails and tacklings, all of which had suffered damage. It was then that our general decided, and the captains were in agreement with him, that the fleet should ply to seaward, and abide there until the sun and the winds dispersed still further the ice within the strait. This was done, whereupon all of the ships took in their sails and lay adrift.

On 7 July, having been carried well out to sea by the tides and the currents, we made sail and worked back in toward the land. But on coming close up to it, arguments arose as to where we really were, as men who had been on the previous voyages professed their willingness to swear they had never before laid eyes on that coast. Fogs which prevented our taking the height of either the sun or Polaris [the North Star], and currents so strong they would turn the ships completely about, added to our uncertainty and confusion. We had thought ourselves to be on the northeast side of Frobisher's Strait when, instead, it had begun to appear much more likely we had been carried, and well, to the southwestward of Queen's Foreland.

Under these puzzling circumstances the general took counsel with his captains and masters, no two of whom seemed of the same mind. However, Christopher Hall, chief pilot of the voyage, plainly and loudly declared we were lying off a strange coast. For the moment, the matter rested there. On 10 July the weather was still so thick no sighting could be taken and, because of that same thickness, some of the ships had become separated from the main fleet. Among the missing ships were the *Thomas Allen*, the *Anne Francis*, and two others whose names cannot be recalled. The remainder of the ships, following the lead of the general, sailed in a westerly direction, proceeding for a distance, or so some will affirm, of as many as sixty [180 miles] leagues. During all of that time they had land to starboard of them and an open sea before.

It was about then that the general agreed, in his own mind, that another strait entirely had been entered. In this respect he later confessed that had it not been for the gold ore with which he was expected to freight his ships, he might have remained in the newfound strait and pursued it clear through to the South Sea and by so doing dissolved all doubt of a passage to the rich country of Cathay. He finally gave orders that all of the ships were to turn back and seek the true strait, namely Frobisher's Strait. An easterly course which kept them within sight of the coast which forms the backside of the supposed continent of America, had them back and lying off Queen's Foreland by 21 July. But once again dense fogs caused the ships to lose sight of each other, and become so separated and scattered, that it was 27 July before they managed to reunite off Hatton's Headland, which headland is a part of Queen's Foreland.

During this time of peril and uncertainty many men lost heart. Some even forgot themselves so far as to speak out loud and say they would as leave return home and face the prospect of hanging as remain in the region and perish amid the ice. However our general, though he was aware of the discontent, closed his ears and persisted in trying to work the fleet back into Frobisher's Strait. While he was endeavouring to do this, there came such a fall of snow, accompanied by a bitter wind, that for hours no ship could see its neighbour. A full six inches and more of snow lay upon our hatches. The poorest of our seamen, those lacking sufficient clothing to keep changing into dry ones, were soaked to their skins and remained in that miserable state so that many fell ill. Some died.

Notwithstanding the difficulties created by the great storm, our general, the moment the weather permitted, once more set about leading his fleet into the true strait. After surviving many perils, he brought nine sail to anchor in the Countess of Warwick Sound on 31 July. However, just when he thought all dangers overcome, his very own ship struck so hard on an island of ice that her anchor fluke [point] was driven through her bows. From the mishap such a leak resulted that it was only by the greatest efforts of her men that the ship was kept from sinking. However, good fortune came mixed with the bad. To the immense joy of all, two ships long missing and believed lost, the *Michael* and the *Gabriel*, were perceived riding safely at anchor in the sound. Unable to rejoin us due to the ice and the weather, but knowing our general intended bringing the fleet into the sound, they had, on their own, preceded us there. In celebration each ship shot off, in the manner of the sea, its greatest ordnance and Master Wolfall, a learned man who had been appointed by Her Majesty's Council as minister and preacher, held a service of Thanksgiving.

Having succeeded, by dint of great effort, in assembling most all of his ships in one place, and that place close by the supposed gold ore, our general that same day summoned all of his captains, and masters too, to a meeting aboard his own ship, the *Aide*. This he did so discussion might be held as to how best to proceed toward freighting the ships with the ore. The following day, 1 August, as had been agreed upon, the various captains put ashore upon the Countess of Warwick Island as many members of their companies as could be spared without endangering the ships. Tents, bedding, victuals, as well as tools for mining of the ore were also landed. In great good order each man was assigned his task, so that the miners were at work even as the soldiers and mariners were erecting the tents.

On 9 August the general again had his captains and masters together, on this occasion so that a decision might be reached regarding the erection of a house, or fort, upon the island from the materials, still at hand, which had not gone down on the *Dennis*. However, it was then revealed that various parts of the intended fort, aside from those lost with the *Dennis*, were missing. It was strongly suspected some of the parts had never left England, while still others had either been damaged or broken when used, as fenders, during the great storm. As a further discouragement the carpenters, upon their being told they must erect a smaller dwelling than planned from the materials still available, loudly insisted that such a task would take them at least two months. The carpenters having spoken their minds, it was the turn of the captains. Some of them raised their voices also. They said that to remain longer than four weeks in the region would be utter madness. So it was that the thought of building a house of any kind was given over, even though Captain Fenton very bravely offered to remain in the land, keeping with him a much smaller number of men than the originally intended one hundred.

Meantime, those ships which were still missing from the main fleet, namely the *Anne Francis* under Captain Best, and the *Thomas* of Ipswich under Captain Tanfield, as well as a flieboat [flyboat; a flat-bottomed vessel], the *Moon*, under command of Master Upcot, had been making divers efforts, though without avail, to rejoin the fleet. They had, however, been successful in remaining in contact with each other. On 8 August the three captains met aboard the *Anne Francis* to decide what course of action should be followed. On more than one occasion the opinion was expressed that the venture should be given over, the reason given that more than likely all of the other ships had perished. Captain Best finally decided the matter, by forcefully declaring that to set course for England would be dishonourable, and indeed could be likened to outright cowardice. He then, as senior captain, ordered the other ships to stay close to his. Notwithstanding his order, the *Thomas* of Ipswich stole away that very night and set course for England.

Undaunted by the desertion, Captain Best proceeded with plans already made, which plans entailed finding a suitable harbour in the vicinity of Hatton's Headland, as well as an island, if such were to be found, which had an abundance of the gold ore. Once safely into a harbour, it was his intention to have his carpenters work on fitting together a pinnace of five tons burden which was carried in the hold of the *Anne Francis*. With those matters in mind, he himself went in a skiff in among the islands under the headland. After diligent searching, he found what he sought: a harbour of good dimensions, the same being nearby an island so rich in the ore it should have satisfied all the gluttons in the world. The island he named after himself: Best's Blessing.

The following day, 10 August, he succeeded in bringing both ships to harbour, but despite a boat's leading the way and taking soundings, the *Anne Francis* struck so hard against a rock she began to take water in such alarming fashion no fewer than 2,000 strokes of the pumps were required to keep her afloat. A further cause for apprehension: when the tide was on ebb, she listed dangerously and threatened to capsize. Only by bringing down her mainyard, and other measures as well, was this prevented. At the next flood, by God's grace, she floated free, whereupon both mariners and carpenters set to work at repairing the leak. While they were about that very necessary task, the miners were beginning to mine the ore. At the first moment carpenters could be spared from working on the leak, some were put to assembling the pinnace. They at once ran into difficulties. When its parts were brought up out of the hold it was quickly discovered that someone back in England had neglected to include the knees [braces], and as though that were not sufficiently bad, there was also a grievous shortage of nails with which to join the planks. However, by grace of God, there was a man among them who was a [black] smith and this man, though lacking the most of the necessary tools of a smith, was undiscouraged and made do with other things. For an anvil he employed a gun chamber; for a sledge hammer he chose a pickaxe, and for lack of a great smith's bellows two small ones were used. Lastly, as small pieces of iron were not to be had, the clever fellow broke up and then heated and made into nails various tools: tongs, gridirons, and even shovels.

On 11 August Captain Best, in company with the ship's master and some seamen, ascended the highest point of Hatton's Headland, doing so for two reasons: First, from its prominence he wished to see how much ice there was in the seas thereabouts; secondly, he wished to erect a cross of stones. Those things were accomplished. It was seen that there was much drift ice in all directions; erecting the cross presented no difficulty as there were plenty of stones, some of them very prettily coloured.

On 17 August a white bear tried to attack the miners as they worked ashore. It was shot and killed and its meat provided a welcome change of fare. The following day, 18 August, the carpenters completed the pinnace, though they warned the captain it was not so strong as it might be due to their having had to fashion knees for it from materials they deemed unsuitable. Indeed, one of the carpenters was heard to say he would have to be given at least £500 before he would trust his own life to that same pinnace. Disregarding the carpenter's opinion of its seaworthiness, Captain Best announced his intention of using the pinnace to see if he could make contact with the other ships of the fleet which, in his judgement, had gone back into Frobisher's Strait. When he asked for men to accompany him, it is a truth there were some who were not eager, but eighteen came forward. Captain Upcote of the *Moon* was one.

The next day, 19 August, with a fortnight's victuals aboard the pinnace, Captain Best and his company departed, but from the outset things did not go well for them. An utter calm had the men rowing for upwards of thirty leagues. However, by dint of oars and sail, they entered into the strait and proceeded upward of it for as many, or so some thought, as forty leagues. This was not accomplished without danger.

Their closest brush with death came when a sudden blow, to say naught of great quantities of drift ice, forced them to seek shelter amid the dangerous rocks and broken ground of Gabriel's

Island. By God's grace, though, they came to no harm and on 22 August—they were by then in the Countess of Warwick Sound—a party which had landed and gone to the top of a hill perceived from afar the smoke of a fire. Taking again to the pinnace, they approached closer to the fire, but were not of a mind to land near it; they could see no ships and so were led into supposing the fire could just as well belong to people of the country. But on going still closer in, an ensign fashioned after the English custom was waved at them by people ashore. Convinced that the flag, if not the persons waving it, was ours, Captain Best resolved to land. If savages, he said, had an English flag in their possession he would recover it even at the cost of his life.

However, while the pinnace was still some distance out it became plain the people gathered on the shore were Englishmen. The meeting was joyful, with backs clapped, caps thrown into the air and muskets fired. The pinnace had come upon a party of miners who were engaged in gathering ore which the ships would call for at a later date. Having learned all this, Captain Best and his men set out toward the place in the sound where the fleet was supposed to be lying at anchor. Captain Best was most anxious to consult the general; he was also desirous that the goldfiners make tests upon the ore samples he had brought with him from Best's Blessing. There was once again great rejoicing when the pinnace arrived at where the fleet lay, with some of the ships shooting off their ordnance in celebration, for it had been thought, by most, that the *Anne Francis* and the other missing ships had been lost.

Captain Best and his men were received aboard the *Aide* by the general himself, who immediately put goldfiners to work at testing the ore. When the goldfiners declared the ore not so rich as that with which the ships were being loaded, the general ordered Captain Best to return to his ships and to bring them, with all haste, back so they could rejoin the fleet. The pinnace at once began the return journey.

On 24 August the general, with two pinnaces and a goodly number of well-armed men, went to Bear's Sound for the express purpose of encountering, and apprehending if possible, some of the people of the country as he was most anxious to take a few of them back to England with him. At various times boats of the people, some so large they contained as many as a score of men, had ventured close in to where parties of our miners were working. But they had steadfastly avoided holding conversation of any kind, and whenever a ship would appear they would flee. On this occasion our general thought, by means of the two pinnaces, to land parties of men on either side of an island they were known to inhabit. It was his hope that as the people fled from one party they would be met by the other. His plan came to naught. Our boats were still a long way from the island when the people were seen to take to their own boats and flee. It would seem they had been keeping constant watch from the top of a high mountain.

On 30 August the *Anne Francis,* which Captain Best had brought from Hatton's Headland, was brought aground so that the greatest of her leaks could be properly mended. That same day, also a house, a small one made of stones and lime, which the general had ordered built on the Countess of Warwick Island, was completed. It was never intended that anyone should inhabit this dwelling. It had been expressly erected so that, the next year, when the place was revisited it would be learned if such a house could resist the heavy snows and deep frosts of the region and remain unbroken. There was an added purpose in leaving such a house behind us. In order that the people of the country might feel better inclined toward us, gifts were left in the house, items such as coloured beads, bells, knives, looking glasses and other small things including pipes. Too, lead engravings of English scenes were hung from the walls, which scenes depicted men and women, and horses being ridden. Last, an oven was made from bricks. Bread was baked in this oven and left so that the people might taste of the food of civilized people.

Nearby this house we buried the timbers which would have gone into our fort had the *Dennis* not been lost. As a final measure, a patch of soil was tilled; in it we planted peas, corn, and other grains. We knew, due the lateness of the season, these grains would not sprout nor grow until the following spring; it was our hope, though, they would be discovered growing when next we came, thus proving the goodness of the ground.

The miners having by then gathered such quantities of the ore as it seemed could safely be put aboard the ships, the general once more gathered together all of the captains, and the gentlemen too. He informed them he was still most desirous of making a further search, upwards of the strait, in the hope a passage through to the Sea of Sur might be found. The captains—while some did indeed offer themselves to such a venture—were, in the main, opposed to any delay or undertaking which might further endanger either their ships or their men. They gave as reasons for their reluctance to tarry the continual mists and fogs, the snow which fell daily, and the frosts which each night were causing ice to form about the ships. They also did not neglect to point out to the general that both food and water were scarce and, too, that various men had already died and others were on their beds.

The general gave a good ear to all of their arguments, and then charged the captains to get their allotments of ore under hatches as quickly as possible and make ready to leave. He also presented to each captain a list of articles pertaining to their conduct and the courses the ships should set on the return voyage to England. On 31 August such ships as could made sail and departed from the Countess of Warwick Sound. Ships which could not leave included the *Anne Francis* and the *Judith*. They were taking on fresh water but would, if possible, attempt to rejoin the main fleet the following day. The fleet at that time would be lying athwart Bear's Sound, awaiting the general who had gone to shore on an island, with numerous men, to hasten the loading of the two barks, the *Gabriel* and the *Michael,* as well as the much larger ship, the *Emmanuel,* a busse of Bridgewater.

The following day, 1 September, Captain Best of the *Anne Francis* put off in his pinnace to bring aboard those of his men who were still ashore. But the wind chose that time to rise, doing so with such violence all plans went by the board. The *Anne Francis* was forced out to sea and Captain Best had, therefore, to be content to spend the night aboard the Bridgewater ship. The general and his men, in no better circumstances, had to board the *Gabriel.* This was not good as the twenty-ton bark was then badly over-overcrowded. All hoped that by morning the gale would die and they could return to their own ships. Instead, morning saw the gale stronger, the seas mountainous, and the main fleet, and the *Anne Francis* too, gone from sight.

Judging that the ships still in Bear's Sound could do naught to assist each other, the general put to sea in the *Gabriel,* and in that bark finally regained his own ship, the *Aide.* Of the two ships remaining in the sound, the busse was in the greater danger. A large ship, she had cast anchors for safety's sake in broken ground with rocks all round. She dared not try moving, so long as her anchors held, for fear of going onto the rocks and foundering. Thus it was that Captain Best was faced with a most difficult choice, or rather choices. Should he remain with the busse, which ship stood small chance of staying afloat? Or should he ask the *Michael* to tow his pinnace out to sea in the hope he could come up with his own ship, the *Anne Francis*? Trying to regain her in the pinnace would have been madness. The poorly built pinnace was threatening to come to pieces. Nor could he take his men aboard the bark; the bark was already overladen.

In his extremity he resolved to commit himself, and his company, to God and the sea. At the stern of the bark, the pinnace was towed many miles until, at length, they spied the *Anne Francis* under sail and hard under their lee [close downwind]. The sight of her was no small comfort, for had they not come up with her many would have perished, not alone from lack of victuals, but from lack of room on the *Michael*. The pinnace was loosed so she could go on her own to the *Anne Francis*, but so damaged and weakened was she that she shivered and sank, taking many of the men's belongings with her, even as those same men were boarding the ship. The master of the *Anne Francis* was commended for being a dutiful man. Out of regard for his captain, and loyalty to the general, he had not tried to get out to sea but had, instead, held his ship in a dangerous road all through the stormy night.

Each and every ship had difficulty during the storm. They became scattered, with each setting its own course toward home. Yet, thanks be to God, all arrived safely in England, some in one port and some in another, about 1 October. Most marvellous of all was the appearance of the busse of Bridgewater, a ship all had regarded as lost.

There died, in the whole fleet, during this voyage, not over forty persons, a small number considering how many ships were in the fleet.

More than 1,000 tons of iron pyrites were taken back to England, only to be dumped into a harbour where they remained until recent years when they were finally dredged up. How could goldfiners have examined samples of the pyrites, again and again, and still say they were rich in gold? In the sixteenth century gold was not a mysterious substance. Gold coins were in common use. The Queen herself, who is reputed to have had a nose for gold, ordered the ore examined and was told it was genuine.

Apparently Frobisher, from first to last, believed the ore was valuable. His belief cost him a considerable amount of his own money. Too, it has been pretty well established that Queen Elizabeth at least partly believed the ore contained gold, and that she, too, contributed, and lost, money in Frobisher's ventures.

Martin Frobisher, so far as is known, never lost favour with the Queen. In the fight with the Spanish Armada he commanded one of the squadrons of English ships. The Queen knighted him. He was still in her service when, in 1594, he successfully led an assault against a Spanish fort at Brest but was wounded and brought back to Plymouth where he died. St. Andrew's parish church in that city has this entry in its register:

November 22nd (1594) Martin Frobisher, knight, being wounded at the fort built against Brest by the Spaniards, deceased at Plymouth this day, whose entrails were here interred, but his corpse was carried hence to be buried in London.

The first voyage of

John Davis

as told by Master John Janes

The exact date of John Davis' birth is unknown, but it is thought to have been about 1550; the place he was born was Sandridge, about three miles from Dartmouth in Devonshire. Davis is best known for the three voyages he made westward in search of the Northwest Passage. On the last one, according to his *Traverse Book,* he worked his way northward, up to the strait between Greenland and Baffin Island that bears his name, to 72° 12′ north latitude. The date was 30 June 1587. On that day he wrote in *The Discourse:* "Since the 21 of this month I have continually coasted the shore of Greenland, having the sea all open toward the west, and the land on the starboard, east of me. For the last four days the weather has been extremely hot and calm, the sun being 5° above the horizon at midnight. The compass in this place varies 28° toward the west."

Davis was one of the most skilled and knowledgeable navigators of his day. In 1594, at his own expense, he published an eighty-page booklet entitled *The Seamen's Secrets.* In it Davis made plain he understood thoroughly such complex things as great circle sailing and magnetic variations. However, like most others of his day, he thought the earth was stationary; he was not aware that the Magnetic Pole keeps shifting. Davis was also hampered on his voyages by the lack of an accurate sea clock, or chronometer. As a result, some of the positions given in the accounts of his voyages are woefully in error as to longitude. Nevertheless, for more than a century, Davis' book was a sort of handbook to navigators. It went into eight editions, the last being published in 1657.

As well as attempting to discover the Northwest Passage, Davis made a voyage to the Strait of Magellan. He was captain of a ship called the *Desire*, one of a fleet of three under the famous privateer, Captain Cavendish. The account of that voyage, one of the horror stories of the sea, is found on page 151. Davis also made voyages to the East Indies. On his last voyage, begun in 1605, he was slain by pirates off the coast of Malacca in present-day Malaya.

Master Janes who supplied this narrative for Hakluyt was a one-time servant to William Sanderson, the man most responsible for arranging for this voyage and for placing Davis in charge. Janes sailed in the *Sunshine* with Davis.

Certain Gentlemen of the Court, as well as divers merchants of London and the West Country, consulted together on the likelihood of the discovery of the Northwest Passage, an enterprise which had been attempted before but had unhappily been given over because those engaged in the action had allowed themselves to be turned away from their original purpose. The gentlemen and the merchants, having debated the matter at great length, decided to supply the necessary shipping. They further agreed to entrust the handling of the entire affair to Master William Sanderson, a merchant of London. Master Sanderson had been foremost in arguing that the venture should be undertaken; he was also the one most generous with his purse. Master Sanderson at once commended to the company that a certain Master John Davis, a man well grounded in the art of navigation, should be made captain and chief pilot of the intended exploit. He was given his way.

The same Master Sanderson having seen to it that everything was put in readiness, we departed from Dartmouth, on 7 June

1585, in two barks. One of these barks was of fifty tons burden and was called the *Sunshine* of London; the other was of thirty-five tons and was named the *Moonshine* of Dartmouth. In the *Sunshine* we had twenty-three persons, some of whose names are as follows: Master John Davis, captain; William Eston, master; Richard Pope, master's mate; Master John Janes, and others. As well, we had a gunner, a boatswain, a carpenter, a cook and a ship's boy. The remainder were seamen, four of whom had been chosen because they were also musicians.

The *Moonshine* of Dartmouth had nineteen persons. Master William Bruton was her captain; John Ellis her master.

The day following our departure the wind came at us so strongly from the west-southwest, that we were forced to put into Falmouth. We lay there for five days. On 13 June the wind became more favourable, blowing from the north, so that we once more put out to sea. But the very next day a wind which was both adverse and strong, drove us to seek shelter among the Scilly Isles [off the western tip of Cornwall]. Undaunted, we ventured forth the following morn. Again we were driven back, this time to harbour in New Grimsby, where we lay for twelve days.

During those twelve days, Captain Davis had the master and me go about with him, so we could assist him, while he charted the coastlines of the islands, as well as certain rocks and harbours. Such information appearing on charts will be of great value to pilots. On 28 June, in God's name and with a fair wind, we departed New Grimsby.

On 1 July while on a westerly course we saw great numbers of porpoises, which caused Master Eston to call for a harpoon. Twice he shot and missed. On a third shot he struck a porpoise in the side, wounding it deeply. When we had it aboard, Master Eston said it was a darliehead. The day after, we ate some of it; it was sweet as mutton. Two days later we again had porpoises about the ships in vast numbers. Master Eston again shot harpoons at them but this time it was to no avail. The porpoises were so large they broke two harpoons, which were all we had. Master Eston, though, decided to continue the sport by casting pikes at the porpoises. He struck one. But as had happened to the harpoon, the pike was broken and the fish went its way. Being a determined man, Master Eston took a boat hook and with it managed to make a strike. When that porpoise also got away, the sport was given over.

Most everyday from then on, as well as porpoises, we saw pods [schools] of great whales.

On 19 July we fell in with a great whirling tide which set to the northward. After sailing about a half a league we passed through it and came to a calm sea. A mist and fog chose that time to descend upon us, with the weather becoming so thick we could not see one ship from the other, even though we held them within fathoms of each other. It was while we lay there becalmed and fog-shrouded, that we heard a mightly roaring noise, as though it were the breaking of heavy surf against a rocky shore. Captain Davis became concerned that a tide might carry us into danger so he ordered a boat hoist out so that it might take soundings. The men in the boat cast their lead, and reported that they could find no bottom even at 300 fathoms. At that, Captain Davis, Master Eston and I went down into the boat and went off in it to see if we could discover the cause of the noises. Before our departure, though, Captain Davis gave the gunner strict orders that he should shoot off, when each half-hour glass had run, a musket in order that we should know at all times exactly where the ships lay.

As we rowed into the fog, the noises increased, and shortly thereafter we met with so many islands of ice that before we knew it we were surrounded by them. We landed on a large piece and it was then we learned that the roaring noises were being made by the ice islands jostling and bumping each other. As we made no haste and so were overlong in doing all this, those on the ships grew fearful that some mishap had befallen us. In their anxiety they not only kept firing muskets, but took to shooting off falconets [light cannon] as well. But we were quite safe. We put their minds at ease by returning, before nightfall, with our boat laden with chunks of ice, which ice would make fresh drinking water. Once back aboard, Captain Davis gave orders that we try working the ships to the northward, in the hope that by doing so we could double the icefield.

On 20 July the fog lifted. When it did, we discovered we were lying off a land which was the most deformed, rocky, and mountainous, any one of us had ever seen. Its mountains were very high and snow-covered, while a league and more out from its shore islands of ice crowded and jammed against one another, making grinding, crunching noises. In all, it presented such a scene of utter bleakness our captain named it, and rightly so, the Land of Desolation [southern part of Greenland]. The next day, 21 July, there came a strong wind from the north. We were driven southward by it until, before we realized, we were in a deep bay. What was more, we were completely surrounded by ice islands. We immediately set to work to get ourselves out of both the bay and its ice; we succeeded, even though it took us all of the remainder of the day and part of the night as well. Upon our reaching more open water, we set our course to the south-southwest, running along the shore.

In the morning, the captain had a boat lowered and, taking six seamen, set out toward the land. His reasons for doing this were: the previous evening, just before darkness had fallen, the water close in to shore had given the appearance of being free from ice; too, various of the seamen had declared they had sighted what appeared to be a canoe being rowed along the shore. As the ships, at the time of the boat's departure, were well out, Master Eston decided he should make sail and follow the boat closer in to land. He need not have bothered, for the boat did not get very far. While still a league from shore it encountered so much drift ice it was deemed useless to proceed, a circumstance which greatly disappointed the captain and his men. However, as seals had been seen and seabirds were beating the water, the mariners were encouraged into thinking that fish should be in good supply. With the captain's permission, the oars were rested while the men dangled lines over the sides. Their efforts were for naught. But while they were engaged in their fruitless pastime, they did much gazing toward the land, with the result that some were again willing to swear they could see trees growing. Others were equally as loud in declaring they could see no trees whatsoever. That is the way of seamen. It could well be, though, that trees do grow in that region, even as they do on Newfoundland, for scarce a day went by when we did not come upon floating trees. On one occasion the *Moonshine* took from the water an entire tree which was full sixty feet in length, fourteen hands [a hand is four inches] in circumference, and it still had all of its roots attached to it.

When the boat crew had grown weary of trying to catch fish where there were none to catch, the boat put back to the ship, and once it and its men were aboard we bent our course southward, hoping thereby to double the land, but we made little headway due to the calmness of the weather. On 23 July we were still coasting the land which stretched from the east-northeast to the west-southwest. On 24 July we were doing likewise but the land then ran in an east-west direction. We were unable to approach it by reason of the great quantities of ice which lay between it and us. The weather at the time was not so chill, with the air somewhat as it is in England at mid-April, but when the wind blew from off the ice it was much colder and far from pleasant. That day, as the mariners were rather downcast, the captain and the master decided to increase their food allowance in the hope it would encourage them. They ruled that, henceforth for breakfast, each mess of five men should have an extra measure of beer, as well as a half pound of bread.

On 25 July we departed the region, losing sight of the land at six of the clock in the morning. Our course was directed to the northwestward; our hope was that God, in His mercy, would guide us to the desired passage. That same course we held for four days.

On 29 July we sighted land in latitude 64° 15′, bearing northeast from us [Gilbert's Sound]. We bore up to it without difficulty as the seas were free of ice and the weather fair and warm. Coming very near to the land we saw it had many deep inlets, as well as fair sounds [deep inlets] and good roads [harbours] where a ship might lie in safety. We brought the bark close up to an isle, moored her to rocks and went ashore hoping to find wood and fresh water. We had no sooner landed than we came upon signs that people had been there, for we found a small shoe and some pieces of leather which had been sewn together with sinews. On another islet close to that one, we also went ashore and the captain, the master, and I went to the top of a high point of rock. We were no sooner atop it than we heard cries and screechings which, at first, we thought must be the howling of wolves. When the cries ceased, I gave a halloo. A human voice returned it! This caused us to look well around us; when we did, we discerned a number of people standing on the beach of an islet some distance from the one we were on, while a canoe was being rowed about another small island close by.

We began to make a great deal of noise, partly to lure the people to us, and partly to warn the members of our own company. Upon hearing our cries, Captain Bruton and Master Ellis of the *Moonshine* lowered a boat and hastened toward us. But to do this they had to pass close to the *Sunshine,* which gave them the idea they should bring our four musicians along with them. Their purpose in doing this was, as they explained later, that the musicians could assist in rescuing us, if that proved necessary, or by playing on their instruments they might attract and please the people of the country. We were in no danger so the musicians at once began to play while the rest of us took to leaping and dancing. We also made various gestures which we hoped the people would regard as signs that we wished to be friends with them.

In this manner we convinced them we meant them no harm so that before too long, from various islands, ten canoes appeared, with two coming close to the shore of the isle we were on. We tried conversing with the occupants of those canoes closest in but it was to no avail. We could not understand each other. At length one of the people took to pointing at the sun with his hand, after which he would strike his chest such a hard blow we could hear it. When he had done this several times, we reasoned it was some sort of friendship sign which he expected would be returned. Arriving at that conclusion, Master Ellis of the *Moonshine* was appointed to be our spokesman. Master Ellis, as had the native, pointed first to the sun and then struck himself a mighty blow on the chest. When he had done this several times, the trust of the people was gained. One brought his canoe in and stepped ashore. To him we tossed, as gifts, caps, stockings, gloves, and other items we had with us which we thought might take his fancy. Finally, we bade them farewell and went aboard. As it was by then late evening, we lay there overnight.

The next morning early, thirty-seven of the one-man canoes came rowing by our ships, with all of their occupants making signs and calling to us that we should go on shore. When we made no haste to comply, one of them went onto the isle we had been on the day before and, going to the top of the high point of rock, he began to leap and dance. He also waved a sealskin at us and began to beat on a thing shaped like a timbrell [tambourine] which made a sound, when struck by a stick, very much like a drum. We lowered our boats then and went to them, but they stayed in their canoes until all of us had sworn, after their fashion, by the sun. Only after we had done that did they trust us. I shook the hand of one and he kissed my own in return. All of them became so friendly that on that particular day we could have had, simply by asking, anything belonging to them. We bought five of their canoes and some of the clothing from their very backs, which clothing was made from the skins of seals and birds. We bought as well buskins [mukluks] which reached to just below the knee of the wearer, and were made from the hide of some beast whose wool was not unlike that of the beaver. We saw among those people leather cured as finely as English glovers do theirs. They even allowed us to take into our hands their darts and their oars. We found them well made, which led us to believe they must have among them many good artificers.

It was most interesting to see the care they took of each other. When we bought a canoe the owner would still be in it. But two of his fellows would immediately come in their canoes and carry the man off between them. They are, or so we judged, a tractable people, devoid of craftiness and very civil, even though they be idolators and worshippers of the sun.

During our stay at those islands, we found and took aboard a reasonable amount of wood. This wood, which was of fir, spruce, and juniper, had all come drifting to there, but whether from far or from near we had no way of knowing. Some of our company were of the opinion that trees must grow not too far distant because the people appeared to be well supplied with wood, not only for making their oars and their weapons, but for framing some of their boats. Along that coast there appeared to be an abundance of seals, which school together much as though they were fish. We searched diligently for either streams or springs of fresh water; finding none we had to content ourselves with replenishing our butts [casks or barrels] from pools of melted snow water.

It is a rocky, rugged land and its cliffs seemed to be all of the same ore Martin Frobisher brought back with him from Meta Incognita. As well, we saw much Muscovy glass [mica], some of which shone like crystal. As for the plants of that place, we found growing upon the rocks a herb whose fruit was sweet and full of red juice [currants]; birch and willow grow there too but, owing to the severity of the climate, they remain as shrubs low to the ground. The people live by the hunt and therefore have great stores of furs. Once they found we would exchange items of our own for those furs, they made signs they would go into the country and return the following day with vast numbers of pelts. This they set about doing. But that night a fair wind came and the captain and the master refused to be diverted, for so much as even a day, from the real purpose of the voyage. At four of the clock on the morning of 31 July we set sail. Hours later, the wind fell of and we lay becalmed, but the next day it blew both fair and strong and allowed us to proceed toward the northwest.

On 6 August we discovered land in 66° 40′ of latitude and, as the seas thereabouts were free from ice, we came close to the land [Baffin Island] and anchored in a good road, under a high mount whose cliffs had veins which, picking up the light, shone much like gold. The place where the ships lay we named Totnes Road; the sound encompassing the mount we called Exeter Sound; the mount itself became Mount Raleigh, while the foreland to the north became Diers Cape [Cape Dyer].

Our anchors had no more than splashed into the waters of the road than we spied four white bears on land by the foot of the mount. At first, we did not recognize them as bears; instead, we thought they must be either goats or wolves. But when we had manned a boat and gone ashore, and then discovered they were bears of immense size, we became more than ever desirous of taking them, not alone for the sport of doing so but for their meat. We landed and assaulted them, and right away one came charging downhill at me. My piece [gun] was loaded with hailshot and a bullet; I discharged it from close up, hitting him in the neck. He veered, gave a mighty roar, and took to the water. We followed him in our boat and finished killing him with boar spears. We also killed two other bears that day.

The next morning we went ashore on a small island in the sound and came upon a truly huge bear lying so fast asleep that he did not hear us as we walked close up to him. I aimed my piece but the flint gave no spark, and the weapon did not discharge. The bear heard. He woke, looked at me, then laid his head back down.

I once more took aim and this time shot him in the head. But my bullets appeared only to amaze him. All of us then ran at him and thrust boar spears into him but, despite the spears, he ran toward the water which was not far off. However, upon reaching the water, he turned and faced us. We were close on him and the master hurled a boar spear and struck him in the head. At that, the bear plunged into the sea and swam to a nearby cove. We followed and, after slaying him, we brought his meat and his pelt aboard. To satisfy our curiosity, we measured one of his forepaws. It was fourteen inches from side to side. All of the bears we took there were very fat. As we did not want the fat, we cut it off and threw it away, keeping only the lean.

We departed from Mount Raleigh on 8 August and coasted along the land which stretches in a southwest to northeast direction. The next day, 9 August, our mariners complained of their allowance, claiming it was too meagre, whereupon we took from them their butter and their cheese but increased other items. It was ruled each mess of five men should have four pounds of bread per day, twelve wine quarts of beer, and six fishes. On meat days they were to receive a gill [a quarter pint] more of peas.

On 11 August we came to the most southerly cape of the land, the one our captain had named Cape of God's Mercy [Cape Mercy]. Though the weather was foggy, we rounded the cape and kept coasting this north land. When the fog broke, we saw we were shot well up a passage [Cumberland Sound], or entrance, which was in some places twenty, or even thirty leagues in width. This passage was entirely without the pester of ice and its water was of the exact same colour as that in the Atlantic. This greatly increased our hopes we were in the passage we sought. We sailed northwest into it for as many as sixty leagues, at which time we came to a group of islands clustered in mid-passage but with open water on either side.

The captains and the masters having consulted, it was decided that the ships should separate, one going to the north of the islands; the other to the south. This we attempted to do. But a wind came at us from the southeast, bringing with it such foul weather both ships were forced to seek shelter amid the isles. On 14 August, some of us went ashore in a boat and no sooner had we landed than we came upon signs that people had been there.

We found stones which had been gathered and arranged so as to form a sort of low wall. We also came upon a human skull.

The day after that—we were forced to lie there five days in all—we heard what we thought to be the howling of wolves on one of the islets. We manned a boat and went to the island, intending to kill them. We had no sooner brought our boat up than a number of animals appeared and rushed directly toward us. Certain they were wolves intending to attack us, we fired our pieces, killing two. Our consternation was great when we found about the neck of one of them a leather thong, which told us they were tame dogs, even though their owners were nowhere to be seen. In all there were twenty of those dogs upon that small isle, each as large as a mastiff, with pricked ears and a bushy tail. The pizzle of one we had shot had been pierced and had a bone in it. Travelling farther about the island we found two sleds, made very much as sleds are made in England, except that one was entirely of whalebone. On that same isle we saw larks, ravens, and a kind of partridge.

On 17 August we were once more on land and I came upon what seemed, at first sight, to be an oven of sorts made from stones and rocks. In it were various hand-wrought items, very small but well made. These included a tiny canoe made from wood, a bird carved from whalebone, beads also fashioned from bone and with holes in them so they could be strung on a string, and other toy-like objects. The land itself is very barren, and consists of little other than rock, though some of the rocks are quite pretty as they have veins of divers colours running through them. We found on one of the isles a seal which had been, and not too long before, killed by people; it had been skinned, flensed, and the meat concealed under a pile of rocks to protect it from birds and animals.

That same day Captain Davis, who was still greatly concerned as to the probability of our finding a passage, had us row among and around the islands to make certain sounds passed through between them. In doing so, we sighted to westward of the islands a pod of four whales. Our sighting the whales had the captain and the master believing they may have come from a westerly sea, as we had seen no whales to the eastward of the islands. We had other reasons for supposing we might be in a passage, or strait, leading to a western sea. The water had not changed colour; it was the same as ocean water. Then there were the soundings we had taken. When only about twenty leagues into the passage we had sounded and got ninety fathoms [a fathom is six feet] with a sandy bottom; off the islands it was 330 fathoms. Too, we had gone out into the sound where the pod of whales had been seen and, of a sudden, we came to where two very strong tides, or currents were meeting and battling with each other. One, we thought, could very well have had its birth in a western sea. Lastly, there were the tides: Between the ebb and flow there were as many as seven fathoms and, try as we might, we could not tell whence they came.

Until 19 August we stayed in the shelter of the islands, though Captain Davis made it known that the moment the weather cleared we would proceed with our search. But on 20 August the wind came directly against us, causing the captains to consult with each other as to whether we should proceed or turn back. On 21 August the wind was again adverse, so we departed the shelter of the islands and coasted along the south shore of the passage where we found many fair sounds. There were so many of these sounds and inlets we were quite persuaded that what we were seeing was not a mainland but a multitude of islands. On 23 August the wind came from the southeast, with the weather so stormy and foul that we were forced to seek shelter in a sound on the south shore where we anchored in twenty-five fathoms. A few of us, despite the weather, went ashore. We saw many signs that people inhabit the place; we saw where they had made fires. Too, we came upon a low wall made from stones. We also saw four falcons and Master Bruton took from one of them its prey, which we judged to be some manner of snipe.

On 24 August, in the afternoon, with the wind fair and to our liking, we departed our anchorage intending, by God's grace, to return to England. Two days later we had our last sight of the north land of the supposed passage. Leaving it astern, we directed our course homewards until 10 September when we fell in with the land Captain Davis had named the Land of Desolation. We had hopes of getting ashore there but, though we searched, we could find no decent road or harbour. As evening had come upon us, we put to sea for the night, intending to come back in the following morning. But during the night and the darkness a great storm came, which so separated our ships that we did not see the *Moonshine* for three whole days. However, on 13 September, the weather having become fine again, we came up with her. In consort with her we left the Land of Desolation and set sail for England.

On 27 September we had our first sight of England. But before we could come to harbour another great storm descended upon us so that, during the night, we lost the *Moonshine*, or so we feared. Three days later, 30 September, we reached Dartmouth and found the *Moonshine*. She had come safely in not two hours before.

Place a fair-sized map of Canada's eastern Arctic, plus Greenland, before you and follow Davis' route. In his own writings, Davis says he made a landfall about 500 leagues from the Durseys. This was the coast of Greenland, somewhat to the north of Cape Farewell. "So coasting this shore to the southward, in the latitude of 60° I found it trends toward the west." He states he followed the trend, remaining in the same latitude, for fifty or sixty leagues. The land then stretched to the northward. He had rounded Cape Farewell.

He followed the Greenland coast until he came to a number of islands "in the latitude of 64° or thereabouts." He moored his ships and named the place Gilbert's Sound. It is not on modern maps. They remained there, refreshing themselves, from 29 July to 1 August. Then they set course to the northwest. On 6 August they discovered land in 66° 40′. They anchored, Davis says, in a fair harbour close to a high mountain [Mount Raleigh].

On 11 August, he rounded Cape Mercy and entered Cumberland Sound and, in doing so, repeated the mistake made by Frobisher—he believed the sound or inlet to be a passage.

The trees found floating along the Greenland coast were not native to the area. They had drifted for years across the Pole from Asia. Wood being much easier to work with than bone, the Eskimos placed a high value on the driftwood.

The twenty dogs found, all by themselves, on an island

are easily explained: It was (and still is) the custom of the Eskimos, and northern Indians, to maroon their dogs on islands during the summer months when they were not needed for either hauling the sleds or hunting. There, the dogs were expected to fend for themselves. Most of them survived; some even learned to fish. Duncan Pryde in his book *Nunaga* describes the Eskimos as a practical people. When a dog was not being worked, he was expected to find his own food. If he could not or would not work he was promptly destroyed.

The bones the English seamen found in the pizzles of the dogs had been placed there as a form of birth control.

The second voyage of

John Davis

as told by John Davis

On 7 May I departed the port of Dartmouth, my purpose being to discover the Northwest Passage. With me I had one ship of 120 tons called the *Mermaid;* and two barks, the *Sunshine* of sixty tons burden, and the *Moonshine* of thirty-five tons. As well, there was a pinnace of ten tons which was called the *North Star.*

On 15 June I discovered land in the latitude of 60° under the Pole and in longitude 47° westward from London. The seas there had such a mighty pester of ice there was no hope of landing. In places it lay against the shore for ten leagues. A fortnight later, 29 June, we again discovered land, on this occasion in the longitude 58° 30′ from London and in latitude 64° [Gilbert's Sound]. This land I had been to the previous year and found it to be well supplied with driftwood, and those of its people we had met were of a friendly disposition. I thought it necessary that we bear in to it in order that we might land in a suitable place for setting up a pinnace which, until then, had reposed in pieces in the hold of the *Mermaid.* A small pinnace, it would, in my judgement, prove most useful as a scout as we would be able to take it into places larger boats could not go. The land itself is very high and mountainous, and has along its coast a mighty company of islands, separated one from the other by channels and sounds so that there is no shortage of harbours. All this we had learned the year before. As on the previous voyage, we again found the seas thereabouts entirely free from ice.

Having brought our ships well in among the islands and sounds, we sent out boats to search for shallow water in which to anchor. Shallow water is not easily found in that place; soundings will usually give 300 and even more fathoms. As one of our boats was engaged in taking soundings, it was spied by the people of the country. Several of their canoes came toward our boat, with their occupants uttering loud cries. However, upon their coming close they recognized among our seamen several who had been on the voyage the previous year. Their joy was great. In their canoes they crowded about the ship's boat, speaking in their own tongue and making signs, and pointing to men they remembered.

When I learned the people were glad we had returned, I, together with some of our merchants and seamen, went ashore and took with me twenty knives. We had no sooner landed than they came running to us, embracing us as old friends. There were eighteen of them so I gave to each of them a knife. They offered skins in return, but by signs I made them understand that the knives were meant as gifts. As we were leaving to go back aboard, they made various signs which we took to mean they would come again, the next day, to the same place and that we would continue to be welcome in their country.

The next day, with all possible haste, the pieces of the pinnace were brought up out of the hold and taken ashore to be fitted together. For our purpose we chose an isle which was convenient, not only to the ships, but one which could be easily defended, even though we had little fear of being attacked. During the time it took the carpenters to set up the pinnace, the people came to us in such numbers there were times when as many as 100 of their canoes were about the ships at once. Nor did they come empty-handed. They brought with them seal skins, stag skins, and the pelts of hares. They also forced onto us seal meat, salmon, cod, cured caplin [smelt], and other such fishes and birds, too, as are found in the land.

While the pinnace was still being pieced together, I decided to do some exploring of the nearby land so I sent a boat out one way while I myself took another boat and went in the opposite direction. Besides discovery, I had another purpose in mind: I wished to see for myself the villages where the people lived. Before my departure I gave the most strict command that on no account should injury of any kind be done the people. No gun was to be fired.

The other boat, the one not under my command, came to a village of the people and found tents made from seal skin with a framework of timbers. In those tents were great stores of dried caplin, which is a fish not much larger than a pilchard; they also saw bags containing seal oil, as well as seal skins in tubs being tanned. Too, they saw many little images carved from wood and bone but, remembering well my orders, none of these items was taken. This company journeyed ten miles into the country, at which time they came to a plain which they described as a champion place because it had earth and grass and was, in some respects, not unlike some of our wastelands in England. Too, they went up a river for as many as ten leagues without reaching its source and found this river to be, at its narrowest place, two leagues broad.

I took my company up another river which at first I had supposed was an inlet but which later proved to be a deep bay. After four hours of rowing we reached its end. At that, I divided my company, a half I left with the boat while with the remainder I went four miles into the country. We found nothing worthy of mentioning, save ravens and numerous small birds such as larks and linnets. We returned to the boat, and put off at once for the ships.

On 3 July, I again caused a boat to be manned and, with fifty canoes of the people attending me, went up a sound which the people, by numerous signs, had made me understand they wished me to see. I had agreed to go, in the belief they were going to take me to at least one of their villages. But when we had been travelling for some hours, the people made signs we should land and go into a warm place for the night. We landed and I, accompanied by some of my men, climbed to the top of a high hill so that I might have a good view of the surrounding land. Seeing nothing of interest, we began our return journey to the boat. Various of the people had, during all this time, been following us closely. They were so anxious to assist us that when we would come to a rock which must be gone over, they would help us up it; if it were steep on the other side, they would ease us down.

When we arrived back to where our boat was, and were resting on the shore, I thought to have some of our seamen play games with the people, for I was curious to see how they would fare in such contests as leaping and jumping. My men outleaped them. But when it came to wrestling it was a different matter. We found they had considerable skill at wrestling, and were so strong and nimble they quickly flung to the ground some of the seamen whom we had considered good at that sport.

The playing over with, we decided to return to the ships as the prospect of sleeping on the rocks did not appeal to us.

The following day, 4 July, the pinnace was completed. Though it proved quite a heavy craft, we had no difficulty launching it. At least forty of the people were on hand to assist us. In great good humour, they made the task of getting it into the water a light one. At that time, our men again played games with them; again in wrestling they fared no better than before. That same day the master of the *Mermaid* went onto some islands to gather driftwood, and while he and his company were on one islet they discovered a common grave with numerous people in it. The grave was open, except for seal skins spread over it, which skins were held in place by driftwood timbers laid down in the form of a cross.

During the time while the pinnace was being prepared, we had remained on the friendliest of terms with the people. Some of them were always with us and this gave the opportunity of closely observing, not only the people themselves, but their habits and customs as well. Compared to our seamen, they were of good stature and well proportioned; their feet and their hands, though, are small and slender. As for their faces, they are broad with smallish eyes and wide mouths. Their men are, for most part, unbearded. They have a custom with which we became most familiar: Each time they came to us, as well as each time they left us, each man would point to the sun. That gesture would be followed by his giving a loud cry of "Ilyaoute!" Last, he would strike his breast a blow which could be heard for quite some distance. As for their beliefs, they are idolators. This we knew, for they keep by them a great number of small images which they wear on their persons or keep in their boats. We were of the opinion they worshipped these images. They have among them men who practise witchcraft and cast spells, though the spells, thanks be to God, do not appear to be of any great strength. On 4 July, we had occasion to see some of their sorcerers at work.

On that day we were on shore. A large number of the people were present and one of them, for what purpose we knew not, began and made a long oration. When he had stopped speaking, he began to make a fire in this manner: He took a piece of board which had a small hole bored part-way through it. Into that hole he thrust the end of a round and pointed stick, the tip of which he first dipped in seal oil. Last, he wrapped a thong of leather about the stick and then, in the fashion of a turner, he employed the thong to rapidly twirl the stick. Very speedily, he produced fire. That done, he added bits of moss and turf, the while he uttered words which we believed must be incantations. He also made strange gestures. He then put divers items into the fire which we judged must be in the nature of sacrifices. To none of this did we object. However, when by signs and slight pushings, they made us to understand they wished each of us to stand in the smoke from their witchfire, we resisted and refused to do so. I made motions that one of their number should go into the thick of the smoke and stand there. None would, so I seized hold of one and pushed him into it. At the same time, I ordered a seaman to stomp the fire out and cast the embers from it into the sea. This I had done in order to show them we had contempt for their sorcery.

It was around that time when we learned that these people can be extremely thievish. In particular if anything is made of iron, or has iron in it, they cannot resist the temptation to steal it, and through our desire to remain on a friendly footing with them, we, alas, encouraged them into revealing this viler part of their nature. Their first offence: they tried to cut our cables. When we stopped them from doing that, they cut away the line which held the *Moonshine's* boat to the stern. Items of clothing which the men had washed and put out to air were stolen. The miscreants, despite our watching them closely, stole some of our oars, a caliver, a boar spear, a sword, and various other things both large and small. These dishonest acts so disturbed our mariners, and masters too, that members of our company approached me, saying that for our very safety we should stop being friends with the people as they were naught but a pack of thieves. Acceding to their wishes, I allowed both a caliver and a falconet to be fired in the belief the loud noise would discourage them. It did. They fled with great haste. But they were back within a ten hour and crying, "Ilya-oute!" and entreating us to be friends with them again. We gave in to them and, to show their gratitude, they brought us seal skins and salmon.

From then on, they restrained themselves from stealing most things, but iron they could not resist. Perceiving this, I could but laugh at their simplicity. I also charged each member of the company to allow them no opportunity to get their hands on anything made of metal. I will not venture a guess as to why they should show such an unnatural desire to own such a worthless bit of iron as a single nail. It could only be of use as an ornament; they lack smiths. But then, they are a strange people in many ways.

For instance, they eat a great deal of their meat raw. For weapons, they have darts, as well as bows and arrows, and slings of a sort. They also possess fishnets, which they make from the fins of whales. When first we met them, we believed them to be a peaceful people; later, we learned they are not. Though peaceful toward us, they have wars with other people of the land. Some exhibited old wound scars, while others suffered from fresh, unhealed wounds which, by signs, they told us they had received from enemies.

On 7 July I went in our new pinnace to make a further search of the land. We passed up a very broad river but as we were doing so a strong gale forced us to seek shelter in a cove where we made preparations for spending the night. Taking half of the company with me, I went inland and climbed to the top of a high hill so that I might have a better view of the country thereabouts. I saw only mountains, many of them mighty, so I returned to the boat and ordered some of the mariners to go and gather mussels for our supper. Mussels are plentiful in that region. While the mussel hunters were about their business and the rest of us were idling, we became witnesses to the strangest sight. A mighty whirlwind sucked up a great column of water and, taking it high up into the air, carried it off. That night, with the gale still continuing, we had uncomfortable beds in the lee of some rocks.

The next morning, the storm having died during the early hours, we went forward, proceeding up the mighty river directly into the body of the land, hoping it would prove to be a firm continent. Instead, we found ourselves among numberless islands of varying sizes, and all of them desert [deserted]. After wearying ourselves by rowing up various channels and inlets, as well as sounds, we turned with the intention of returning to ships. But the pinnace chose that time to develop a leak so we put in to an island in order to stop the leak. While some of the men were doing that, others of us went about the island, where we came upon the burial place of some of the people. We also came upon a great store of dried fish in bags; we took one bag and left the others. On 9 July we arrived back at the ships. We found them surrounded by scores of canoes.

No sooner was I up the ladder and aboard than my mariners were complaining most bitterly to me about the people. In angry tones I was told that my leniency toward the people had encouraged them in their thieving ways. "They have stolen an anchor," the mariners said; "and cut our cable! Too, our boats have been cut adrift. Furthermore," they said, "since you have been gone they have taken to casting stones at us from their slings. Some of the stones weigh as much as half a pound. 'Do we,' " they asked, " 'have to put up with such insults?' "

I cooled their anger somewhat, by promising that I would endeavour to make matters right. The next morning, early, I went on shore where I had the people gather round me. I then told them, as best I could and with what courtesy I could, that they must change their ways toward us if they wished us to regard them as friends. In the belief I had succeeded in my purpose, I went back aboard. In their canoes they followed me to the ship's side so I tossed them a few bracelets as gifts. I also made signs that we would welcome a number of them aboard. Eight came up the ladder and we treated them courteously. They showed considerable curiosity about the ship's gear, and when some of them expressed a desire to climb the rigging, we encouraged them to do so. They finally departed.

We believed the matter settled. But it was not. The sun was no sooner down than they were again showing the devilishness of their nature; they were again using their slings to cast stones onto the decks of the *Moonshine*. One of the stones struck the boatswain such a blow he was knocked off his feet. At that, my manner toward them changed completely. In great anger, I ordered our boats lowered but even as they were touching the water the people had guessed our intent. They fled in their canoes. We pursued them and fired several shots at them, though to small or even no purpose. They can row so swiftly they quickly put themselves beyond the range of our muskets.

The next morning, though this may sound beyond belief, five of them were back and behaving as though all was well. My master of the *Mermaid* came to me and said we should entice them aboard and hold all of them prisoner until our stolen anchor was returned. He became most vehement about this when he noticed, among the five, the ringleader and master mischief maker of the lot. When that miscreant cried, "Ilyaoute!" and made the usual gestures signifying he wished only to be our friend, the master replied in like fashion. When the man held up a pair of gloves for barter, the master displayed a knife which he indicated he would exchange for the gloves. Trust was thus established; the ringleader and a companion climbed the ladder and came aboard. Once they had set foot on the deck, the trouble-maker was seized. The other man was allowed to go free.

We at once, and by employing every sign we could devise, made it clear to the people that our captive would be released the moment our anchor was returned. However, though they appeared to understand us perfectly, they made no effort to return our anchor and so, when within the hour a fair wind came, we made sail and departed, taking our captive with us. One of his fellows followed us in his canoe, coming so close astern that he and the prisoner shouted back and forth to each other. While they were conversing, we would, from time to time, point to the prisoner and say, "Ilyaoute." Finally, the fellow in the canoe began to make sounds which to our English ears sounded like lamentations. At that, our fellow shouted four or five words, no more, to his countryman. He then clapped his hands over his face and bowed his body forward and down. The man in the canoe repeated both the words and the gestures. He then gave up following us and went back the way he had come. We judged, both from the words and the signs, that our captive was telling his countryman that henceforth he (our captive) should be regarded as one who was dead.

For some days after being taken, our prisoner appeared to be griefstricken. However, he soon rallied and became a pleasant fellow, and one who was ready and willing to put his hands to a rope and climb in the rigging the same as the mariners. Because he had not been warmly dressed when captured, we fitted him out in English fashion and he appeared to be pleased. The only thing about our ways he did not seem to take to was the fare. He wished to exist, or so it seemed, entirely on raw fish.

During all of this time, for which we were thankful to God, our mariners were in good health, except for one young man. On 14 July he died and the next day, after the customary service, he was cast overboard.

On 17 July we were in latitude 63° 8′. On that day we fell in with a mighty, and strange, mass of ice. It was so vast and had so many high hills, as well as inlets and bays and capes that, viewed from a distance, it had us believing we were looking upon a group of snow-covered islands. So convinced were we of this that we even sent a pinnace to explore it. The pinnace returned to report that what we were seeing was naught but ice. We coasted that mass of ice until 24 July at which time the weather became so wet and cold, and foggy, that our ropes and our sails were coated entirely with ice. I was greatly disappointed as these were the same seas which, the year previous, I had found ice-free and navigable. For another six days, or until 30 July, we sought an opening westward but our search was in vain.

During that fortnight while we coasted the ice mass and endured the foulest of weather, our mariners became discouraged and various of them fell ill. They therefore, though in a very orderly fashion, came to me and entreated me to take into account, not only their safety, but my own. They declared that my overboldness in lingering in the region could earn me bitter curses, not from their lips, but from those of women left widows and children made fatherless. Their mention of widows and orphans caused my conscience to be troubled, but I reminded them of the importance of what we were attempting to do, and that there still remained an excellent chance of our being successful. There was, I said, a way we had not yet tried which could very well lead us to the discovery we sought. Lastly, I warned them it would be to their disgrace, and my discredit also, should we turn aside from our purpose so early in the season.

Having said all of those things, I outlined a plan I had long had under consideration. It was this: The *Mermaid,* albeit a very strong and good ship, was not so suited for working amid islands and ice as was the smaller *Moonshine.* (The other two vessels, on my orders, had long since separated from us.) Too, the *Mermaid* was costing the owners £100 a month. Taking all of those things into mind, I was determined to revictual the *Moonshine* as well as take into her the healthiest and strongest of the mariners and with her continue the action as God should direct me. The *Mermaid* would be allowed to return home by herself. Having made my position known to all, I ordered a change in course, one which took us away from the ice which had been thwarting us. We held to east-south-east so that on 1 August it pleased God to have us discover land in latitude 66° 33′ and in longitude 70° from London. There, the seas were free from the pester of ice and there was no snow on the land either.

On 2 August we harboured in an excellent road where we proceeded, with the greatest of haste, to grave [scrape] the *Moonshine* and revictual her. While the mariners and carpenters were engaged in those tasks, Master Eston went searching in the pinnace but nowhere did he find firm land; islands only did he come upon with seas to east and west and north. The weather at that time was very warm and when Master Eston and his company ventured ashore they found themselves attacked by a fly which is called the mosquito whose sting is grievous. The people of the country were immediately aware of our presence and, as a friendly gesture, they caught a seal, attached bladders to it so it would keep afloat, and sent it drifting to us on the flood. It came right to the ships.

On 5 August I went, with the two masters and others, to the top of a high hill in order to better observe the land lying thereabouts. While about this undertaking, Master Eston chanced to spy three canoes lying by a great rock. We went to the canoes and found in them various skins, as well as darts and a number of toys which we judged must have some superstitious value. None of these things did we bring away with us; instead, we left in each boat trifles such as a small piece of silk, a lead bullet, and a pin. In that way we gained the trust of the people, for the next day they came to us without fear and we bartered with them for skins. We found that in appearance they differed not at all from the other people of that region. Their clothing and their canoes were also the same. In their speech, though, they seemed to form their words more in the mouths, and not so far back in their throats as had the others.

Our savage showed no desire to be put ashore to join them. Instead, with signs he gave us to understand he would like one of them to be a companion to him. We provided him with one and I departed from there on 12 August at six of the clock in the morning. The *Mermaid* we left riding at anchor. On 14 August, sailing westward about fifty leagues, we discovered land in latitude 66° 19′. That same day from nine o'clock at night until three in the morning, we lay moored to an island of ice, which island of ice was about twelve leagues from shore. Departing from there, we sailed southward until 18 August when, in the morning, we discovered land lying to the northwest of us. A fairly high promontory, in latitude 65°, it had no land to the south of it, which raised our hopes of a through passage. In the afternoon of that same day we once more raised land, this time to the southwest and by south from us. That night we lay becalmed. The following day at noon, by observation, we were in 64° 20′, which would lead one into believing we had sailed fifteen leagues south and by west. However, by more exact observation we found our course to be southwest. That caused us to conclude there is a strong current striking to westward. That current, and the fact the land there is nothing but isles, increased our hope of a passage.

On the evening of 19 August it began to snow and continued to do so all night long. There was also much wind which made for such foul weather we were forced to lie ahull about five leagues off shore. On 20 August the weather cleared somewhat so we tried working back in toward the land; at mid-morning we came into a sheltered road where we anchored and felt safe. I at once went ashore and ascended a hill so I could see for a distance. All were islands. At four of the clock in the afternoon we weighed anchor and having a fair wind from the north-northeast, we were free of the land in two hours. We then shaped our course to the south, for the express purpose of searching the coast in the hope that God would, in His mercy, direct us to the passage.

We held on our southerly course until 28 August, at which time we found ourselves in latitude 57° and with a coast to the west of us. We were seeing, by then, incredible numbers of birds, chiefly gulls and mews, and the waters had a marvellous store of fish. Once during a calm we lay for one glass, a half hour, and during that short space our lines brought up 100 cod. Later that same day, 28 August, we became distrustful of the weather and put into a good harbour in latitude 56°. This harbour, which could have been termed a bay, was two leagues broad and so deep we sailed up it for as many as ten full leagues. We found it a fair place; its land well wooded. We tarried there until 1 September because of storms. Despite the storms, though, I landed and went inland for six miles and in so doing observed that fir, pine, alder, yew, withy [willow], and birch grow there. I, and my company, also saw a black bear as well as birds of various sorts, including geese, ducks, blackbirds, jays, thrushes, pheasants, and partridges. With our bows and arrows we killed a great many of the pheasants and partridges. We also tried for fish and discovered that, in particular, by the harbour's mouth, there were many cod.

On 1 September at ten o'clock we made sail and coasted the shore to the southward in fair weather. On 3 September it was close to being calm so we took in our sails, put out a kedge anchor [small anchor], and tried for fish. We were, at that time, in latitude 54° 30′ and cod is in such abundance there that no sooner was a line down than a fish attached itself to it. Besides, they were the the largest and fattest cod any of our company, some of whom had been fishermen, had ever laid eyes upon.

On 4 September at five o'clock in the afternoon we anchored in a very good road amid a group of islands. The country there is low and pleasant, and well wooded. Shortly before coming to anchor in that road we had suffered a keen disappointment; northward about eight leagues we had come upon a wide opening between two lands. We would gladly have gone westward into it but the wind was so strongly against us we had to forego the idea.

We lay in the road for two days, during which time all of the company were busily engaged in either hunting, fishing, or working on the rigging of our bark. On 6 September there came a fair north-northwest wind and we would have departed on the instant, except for one thing: A considerable quantity of fish which we had in mind to cure, had been gutted and split and left on an island over night. Five of our young seamen were sent to fetch the fish. But unknown to us, the brutish people of the country had learned of the store of fish and were lurking in the nearby woods, waiting for us to come and claim them. They made a sudden assault upon our five men. Perceiving this treachery from the ship, we slipped our cable and, with all possible haste, endeavoured to get to the assistance of our men. We also took to firing calivers in the hope the noises would frighten the people away. The sounds did. But not before two of our men had been slain by arrows, and two more grievously wounded. The fifth young sailor, despite an arrow in his arm, had leaped into the sea and swam out to meet us. We landed an armed party and recovered both our wounded and our dead.

That evening, God further increased our sorrows by sending a mighty tempest from the north-northeast. For a space of four whole days this great storm continued; at its height it appeared certain we would be driven onto the rocks, lose our ship, and be at the mercy of the cannibals. At one time, we unrigged the ship and were prepared to cut down our masts. Our anchor cable broke. Yet when it seemed all hope was gone, and we were in the deepest of distress, the good Lord saw and had mercy. We drifted into the lee of an isle where we were safe and protected. We even had the good fortune to recover our anchor.

On 11 September we departed with a fair wind, shaping our course for England. We arrived in the West Country at the beginning of October.

Davis left Dartmouth with four ships: The *Mermaid,* the two barks the *Sunshine* and the *Moonshine,* and a pinnace called the *North Star.* In his own account of the voyage Davis never again mentions the *Sunshine* and the *North Star.* In the above rewritten version, brief reference is made to them for the benefit of the reader to keep him from becoming confused. What became of the two vessels is this: Prior to reaching Iceland, Davis divided his tiny squadron, sending the *Sunshine* and the *North Star* to range northward along the Greenland coast on the offchance they might be able to round it. They were ordered to proceed, if possible, to the height of latitude 80°. After that, they were supposed, by either a northern or southern route, to rendezvous with Davis in latitude 64°—Gilbert's Sound on the west Greenland coast. Davis does not mention this arrangement in his narrative. Nor was the rendezvous ever made. The fate of the two ships, though, is well known. The *Sunshine* returned safely to England; the *North Star* was lost, with all hands, during a storm.

After he parted from the *Mermaid* off the Greenland coast, Davis on the *Moonshine* crossed Davis Strait and again sailed up Cumberland Sound. Because he did not have a chronometer, and because the old sea glasses [sand glasses] were not always reliable, Davis was often several degrees out in his listing of longitudinal readings. For instance, the first position he gave us is for June 15. On that day he states he was in latitude 60°, longitude 47° from London. There can be little doubt but that he was off Cape Farewell on the southern tip of Greenland. His latitude is correct enough; his longitude is out approximately 5°. From London, Cape Farewell lies in about 42°. On June 29 he writes he discovered land in 64° of latitude and in longitude from London 58° 30′. If you look at a map, you will see that according to this reading he was right in the middle of Davis Strait. The land, he says, was "east from us." By his own statement, the land must have been Greenland. Yet the coast of Greenland is close on 6° to the eastward. All of the longitudes Davis gives us appear to be five or six degrees greater than they really were.

The voyage of

The Sunshine and the North Star

as told by Henry Morgan

On 7 May 1586, we departed Dartmouth haven with four sail: the *Mermaid,* the *Sunshine,* the *Moonshine,* and the *North Star.* In the *Sunshine,* which ship I was in, there were sixteen men.

Two days from our leaving Dartmouth, we were off the Isles of Scilly; on the fourth day we were passing by Dursey Head. After that, with Ireland astern of us, our course was northwest, a course we held until we were in latitude 60°. Then it was that our general, Master Davis, decided to divide his fleet. The *Mermaid* and the *Moonshine* would continue to the northwest; the *Sunshine* and the *North Star* would seek a passage northward between Greenland and Iceland. We would search, land and ice permitting, to the height of 80°. He sent us from him on 7 June.

On 9 June we came to a great field of ice which we coasted until 11 June. That same day, at six of the clock in the evening, we saw a land that was very high, and knew it to be Iceland. It lies in 66° and is well peopled. We came to harbour there the following day. The seas surrounding Iceland abound in fishes, and the people take many, including green fish, hake, and a fish they call the scatefish. They also farm and we saw their cattle and sheep and horses and dogs. Their dwellings, which are for most part built close to the sea, have walls of stone and turf-covered roofs.

The boats of the Icelanders are similar to our own in that they are constructed of wood and have iron keels. Too, their fishing and other gear could be mistaken for our own, and the same can be said of most all of their tools and even their household goods. Fishing with these people would appear to be their chief occupation; they dry vast quantities of them and, when they are cured, they store them in the tops of their houses. Were we to go there just to fish in their waters it could be a most profitable venture, as was proven when we, ourselves, took over 100 green fish in one morning. We found on Iceland an English ship which had arrived there at Easter to trade, but would soon be returning to England. It had two owners and one of them, a merchant from Ipswich, came aboard the *Sunshine,* bringing with him two lambs as a gift.

We departed from there on 16 June and set course to the northwest. Shortly after leaving we sighted two small barks but we let them go their way, for we were mindful of the purpose of the voyage and so we held on our own course until the end of the month. On 3 July we found ourselves in between two icefields but were able to stay on course until evening, at which time the master decided to turn back and, once we reached open water, we went toward Greenland. On 7 July we sighted Greenland, seeing it as a very high country, but we could not come to a harbour because of the ice which lay out from the shore for as many as three leagues. Divers days we coasted along that ice until, on 17 July, we sighted the land which Captain Davis had, the year previous, called the Land of Desolation. We could not get ashore for the ice. That night, and the next day as well, we were much troubled by ice but, getting clear of it, we ranged along the coast of Desolation until the end of the month.

On 3 August we came into Gilbert's Sound which lies in [latitude] 64° 15′. It was there we were supposed to rejoin the fleet, but neither the *Mermaid* nor the *Moonshine* were anywhere to be seen. However, at six of the clock in the evening we came to harbour and put out our anchors.

The next morning the master, taking ten men with him, went on shore; when he came back he brought with him four of the people of the country who were, of course, rowing their own boats. In the afternoon I and six men went to the land; seven of the people came to us and while we were ashore we came upon the bodies of three dead people. All three were wrapped in old skins and two had staves lying beside them, as the third did not we judged it must be the body of a woman. We saw some of the houses of the people. They were near the sea and crudely built, being only frameworks of poles covered with turf. We saw foxes running about on the hills, and on the islands too, for the coast there is very broken and consists of little else but isles.

On 21 August the master sent six men ashore to gather driftwood. Perhaps the people did not like our gathering the wood, for thirty-one of them approached our men and began to cast darts at them. Those of us still aboard saw this happening and were fearful our men would be slain so the master at once sent the pinnace in toward the shore. When the people saw the pinnace coming, they turned and fled but the master ordered a caliver shot off anyway. His purpose in doing this was not to hurt any of the people, but only to put fear into them. Many times after that they would wave at us from the shore and make signs they wished us to come and play at football with them. Some of our company finally did go ashore, but when one of the people would approach and try to strike the ball our men would throw him down.

We named the island by where we were anchored, Merchants Isle, and we departed from there on 23 August. Our course was south by west; the wind coming from the northeast. That day and night we ran as many as five or even six leagues. The following morning at eleven of the clock in the forenoon we spied a good harbour and went into it. This new harbour had islands and on some of the islands we could see dogs running about. None of this land has trees growing upon it, but there is no shortage of wood as there is a lot of driftwood. Before we had been there very long four of the people who had visited us in our former harbour came to us, having followed us in their canoes. They gave us some bones, but we could not tell from what beast the bones had come. On the land itself we found great hart [deer] horns, but we did not see any of the stags themselves, though we did see their tracks which were very large. The stones of the country appeared to be worthless, but nevertheless we took samples of them with us.

On 30 August we left there, intending to shape our course for England. We had departed early in the morning. By eleven of the clock a wind which was both strong and contrary had us seeking shelter in yet another harbour. While we lay there, thirty-nine of the people came to us, bringing thirteen sealskins which we got from them in trade. After the dealing for the skins was completed, the master sent our carpenter to change a boat, one we had got from them before, for another. This the people did not like and they would have taken the boat from our carpenter by force. When they saw we would not let them do this, they began to shoot their darts at us. One of our men was struck in the chest. At that, a man of ours, John Filpe, shot one of them in the chest with an arrow. They came at us again, shooting more darts at us, whereupon four of our seamen went into the ship's boat. They seized one of the boats of the people and took its owner into the boat with them. That one had a knife on him. He wielded it, wounding one of the seamen. At that he was slain and cast overboard. We also shot arrows at them so that two more were killed in their boats. They then fled to the shore, taking their dead with them, even the one which our men had cast overboard out of the ship's boat.

Three of them went to the shore which was close by where our ships were lying. They had dogs on that island and one of the dogs leaped into the water and began to swim toward the ships. About then, though, the master ordered our gunner to fire one of our largest pieces toward the people on the shore. The people fled and the dog turned about and went back to the land. From then on they watched us from afar, not daring to come close to us as they had before.

On 31 August we departed Gilbert's Sound, shaping our course for home. As we left the harbour, seventeen boats of the people followed us out to sea for the purpose, or so we thought, of seeing which way we went. On 2 September we lost sight of the land. That night there came a mighty storm which had us lying ahull for many hours. During the storm we lost sight of the pinnace, the *North Star*, and we never saw her again, even though we lay-to all of the next day, tarrying in the hope she would appear. After that we gave up hope and set our course toward home so that, on 27 September, we came in sight of Cape Clear in Ireland.

On 6 October we came safely into the Thames, thanks to God.

It is difficult to trace the course of the two barks after they left Iceland, for Morgan does not give us their latitude when the coast of Greenland was sighted. However, there is some suggestion that they followed, fairly closely, the course taken by Davis on his first voyage. (He arrived off the Greenland coast at, or about 62° north latitude.) After sighting Greenland, they sailed southward. Rounding Cape Farewell they proceeded northward to Gilbert's Sound, where they remained for twenty days, waiting for Davis to appear. When he did not, they set sail for home.

The game Morgan describes as football was quite likely a game the Eskimos call aqraorak. It consists of leaping into the air and trying to kick a sealskin ball dangling from a pole. The game is still popular today. In the Arctic Winter Games held in Whitehorse in March 1972, an Eskimo from Inuvik, Mickey Gordon, came within a "toe" of breaking his own world record of 7′ 2″.

The third voyage of

John Davis

as told by Master John Janes

On 19 May, 1587, at about midnight, we weighed our anchors and set sail from Dartmouth with two barks and a clinker-built pinnace. The barks were the *Elizabeth* of Dartmouth and the *Sunshine* of London; the clinker was the *Helene* of London. The wind, at the time of our departure, was a good fresh gale from the northeast. Within three hours we lost sight of the pinnace, and Captain Davis, believing her men might be taking advantage of the thick darkness to run off with her, ordered the *Sunshine* to stand to seaward for the purpose of sighting the pinnace come morning. In the meantime, we who were in the *Elizabeth* continued on course toward Plymouth.

At daybreak we, ourselves, sighted the *Helene*. Bearing up with her, Captain Davis demanded to know what the trouble was, for it so happened the pinnace was lying ahull. Her master answered, saying the tiller of her helm had broken. It was a bad beginning. However, we reasoned that ofttimes such a beginning has a good ending. Some of our company, though, expressed their doubts regarding the pinnace. The doubters were those who did not favour the way she was built, but as there was little anyone could do about that we placed our trust in God and proceeded on our way. When her tiller had been repaired, the *Helene* followed.

On 21 May, we met the *Red Lion* of London, which was returning homeward from the coast of Spain. Her people feared we were men-of-war, but we hailed them and, after conversing with them, finally convinced them we meant them no harm. We then asked them if they would carry some letters to London for us. They agreed and we heaved them a line, after making fast to our end of it four letters. But our labours and theirs were lost. The letters fell into the sea. Her master then promised that he would certify to certain persons in London that we had departed Dartmouth, whereupon we thanked him and parted from them. Later on in the day we sighted the Scilly Isles. For three days following that the wind was at the northeast and the weather was fair. On 25 May we lay-to, waiting for the *Sunshine* whose company was searching for a leak which had had the mariners at the pumps for 500 strokes during the space of a single watch [four hours].

On 26 and 27 May there was fair weather, but on the latter date the foremast of the pinnace broke and went overboard. On 28 May, the *Helene* had fallen so far behind we held up for her and the *Elizabeth* took her in tow, since she had proven to be a slow sailer unless the wind was brisk. This caused us disappointment as, before leaving England, the owners had bragged about her fleetness, yet once at sea she was much like a cart drawn by an ox. From that day on, whenever the breeze was scant one of the barks would take her in tow. This so annoyed Captain Davis that on 31 May he inquired of Peerson, the steward of the venture, if the pinnace were at all staunch. Peerson replied that, not only was the *Helene* as sound and staunch as a cup, but she took the seas well. This made all of us glad, as it stilled many of our fears.

The first six days of June we had fair weather; after that we had five days of fog and rain, with the wind mostly from the south. By 12 June we again had clear weather. It was then that there was disagreement aboard the *Sunshine*. The mariners went to the master and complained that a promise made them was not being fulfilled. Before leaving England, it was the understanding that the barks would accompany each other, and the pinnace, until Greenland was reached, after which the *Sunshine* and *Elizabeth* would go southward to fish while Captain Davis, in the pinnace, would devote his time to discovery. The mariners argued that the season was wasting, and that if any fishing were to be done it should be done soon. The master of the *Sunshine* listened to all of their arguments, and then told them he would not dream of departing southward to fish, unless it were in the company of the *Elizabeth*. At that, the temper of his mariners was such it caused him to seek an audience with Captain Davis, to whom he voiced his fears that his men might, some time while he slept, change the course of the *Sunshine* and take her away from the other vessels.

However, when the *Sunshine's* men had been threatened and told what would, in the end, happen to them if they did not obey their master, they readily agreed to cease their grumblings and work their ship until such time as Captain Davis should allow it to go fishing.

On 14 June, at five of the clock in the morning, we sighted high, snow-covered mountains which we judged to be about sixteen or even seventeen leagues distant from us. Two days later, at five of the clock in the afternoon, we brought the ships into a harbour. Even as we were letting go our anchors, the people of the country were coming to us in their canoes. As gestures of friendship, they were waving sealskins and crying, "Ilyaoute!" If said in English, that single word would say, "I mean no harm."

The following morning, Peerson and the ship's carpenters landed on an island for the purpose of fitting together the parts of a pinnace Peerson had framed in Dartmouth, out of boards he had brought from London. During the next two days while the pinnace was being built, others of us visited various of the nearby islands in order to learn what we could about them. We found nothing of importance, though we came upon bits of pumice, and also upon rocks encrusted with salt, the salt being so white and pure it glistened. On that same day, the master of the *Sunshine* took a young man of the people who was a strong, lusty fellow.

The next morning, at two of the clock, the savages visited the island where Peerson and the carpenters had been setting up the pinnace and had it all but ready for launching. They set themselves to tearing the boat apart, probably for the iron nails fastening the planks together, and had removed the two upper strakes before they were noticed. Two boats from the *Elizabeth* were ordered lowered and manned and they headed shoreward with the intention of driving the savages away from the pinnace. But the savages, upon seeing the boats approaching, turned the pinnace up onto its side, thus making it a bulwark against the arrows our men shot at them. Seeing that the savages were ready and willing to do battle, our mariners hesitated to land in the fear they might fare badly in an encounter.

Captain Davis was of the same mind and ordered the boats not to attempt a landing. Instead, he told the gunner to load a saker [a small cannon] and to aim it at the upturned pinnace. But when the piece was in readiness for firing, the captain had a second thought. Should the saker be fired, the pinnace would be ruined completely, something the owners would not approve of. He therefore ordered the gunner to remove the cannonball and leave only the powder. When the saker was fired, those of us who did not know the ball had been removed were amazed to see no damage had been done either to the pinnace or to the savages hiding behind it. However, the loud noise frightened them so they retreated in great haste. But as they ran off, they took with them the planks they had removed. They took those planks to an island about two miles distant, where they removed the nails but left the wood. When we saw that the pinnace had been ruined, at least for the purpose for which it had been intended, it was decided that what remained of it should be taken aboard the *Elizabeth,* where later it might be turned into a smaller boat for fishing from.

After this trouble with the people of the country, we resolved to depart the place with the first wind; we would have, too, had we not been visited by another misfortune. John Churchyard, whom Captain Davis had appointed pilot of the *Helene,* came aboard the the *Elizabeth* and reported to the captain and Master Bruton that the clinker was leaking so badly her men had to stand 300 strokes at the pump to keep her afloat, even as she lay in harbour. All of us were disquieted by Master Churchyard's news. Some men were heard to say they would not so much as set foot in the *Helene,* let alone risk their lives in her. However, Captain Davis was firm and said there would be no thought of giving up the venture, or even delaying it on account of a leaky pinnace. He would much rather, he declared, end his life in honour and credit than return home in disgrace. When the captain had spoken so boldly, others of us also stated we would go with him into the *Helene* so, without further ado, we took our belongings aboard the pinnace and, at eleven or twelve of the clock on 21 June, we departed from those isles which lie in 64° of latitude. Once clear of the harbour, we proceeded northward along the eastern shore, which we called the Shore of our Merchants [west coast of Greenland] because there we had met and trafficked with the people.

The two barks departed from there also. They sailed southward toward the fishing grounds of Newfoundland which lie in latitude 54° or thereabouts.

On 24 June, we were in latitude 67° 40′. There we saw a great many whales, as well as seabirds which the mariners said were cormorants. That same day, at six of the clock in the evening, we saw two canoes far out to sea. Upon our first sighting them we thought they were seals, but then we saw the sun being reflected off their oars. They rowed toward us as fast as they could and, when within hailing distance, they rested their oars and gave the usual cry of, "Ilyaoute!" We returned the cry and minutes later they were alongside. We traded bracelets and other trinkets to them for birds. For a knife, I got from one of them a dart which was tipped with what I believed might be bone from the horn of a unicorn. These people followed us for a space of at least three hours.

On 25 June at seven of the clock in the morning, we spied no fewer than thirty savages rowing after us, even though we were at that time all of ten leagues from land. Coming up with us, they produced cured fishes, both salmon and caplin, as well as birds, and these we got from them by giving in return pins, needles, bracelets, nails, knives, looking glasses and other trinkets. We also got twenty skins, but by signs they made us understand that if we would come ashore we could have a great many skins. The trading over with, they followed the ship closely until eleven of the clock at which time, as was our custom, we went to prayer. While we were praying, they left us.

The 28 and 29 June were foggy. On 30 June we took the height of the sun and found ourselves in 72° 12′ of latitude. The sun at midnight was 5° above the horizon; the compass had a variation of 28° to the westward. For nine days prior to then we had been sailing along the land we called the London Coast [Greenland]. To westward and northward of us the seas were open; the land was to starboard, or east of us. On 30 June the wind shifted to the north, whereupon we shaped our course westward and ran for all of forty leagues and better without sighting land of any sort.

On 2 July we fell in with a great bank of ice which lay to the west of us and stretched in a north-south direction. We would have preferred to try doubling this ice by sailing northward, but the wind was so strongly against us we had no choice other than to coast it southward instead. Our purpose, though, still remained the same: to get around the ice so that we might continue on a westerly course. On 3 July the ice bank was still with us; again there was talk we should try to double it to the north. But as on the previous day the wind was against us. On 4 and 5 July there was bad weather with a gale from the north.

On 6 July it was clear, and by gazing westward several members of our company were of the opinion they could see open water. As our intention was still to get to the westward, we sought for, and found, an opening leading into the bank of ice. It was a narrow channel and so we had to resort to oars in order to make headway. After much labour, we decided our eyes had been deceiving us and there was no open water to the westward, so we turned and headed eastward toward the open sea. At midnight of 8 July, by God's help, we accomplished our purpose. On 9 July we lay becalmed. On 10 July we coasted the ice; 11 July we lay becalmed in a fog.

July 12 again found us coasting the edge of the ice, with the wind from the north-northwest. The following day, we determined, if it were at all possible, to get close in to the shore and to anchor in some sheltered road or harbour, to remain there for a week, or longer if need be, in the hope the sun, which was strong, and the winds would dissolve and break up the ice. Should that happen, we would once more proceed with a search of the western shore. We did succeed in getting quite close to the land but we found the water so deep that various of the company were fearful of our attempting to anchor there, so we once more put out to sea. The people of the country, who had been watching us closely, put off in their canoes and followed us, even though the seas were running high, in order that they might trade with us. When they had come up with us, they offered a number of skins which we got from them in exchange for the usual trinkets and pins and needles. They seemed most anxious that we accompany them back to the shore, and kept making signs which we took to mean they would welcome us to their villages. We disregarded their invitations and, bidding them farewell, we departed.

On 14 July the wind blew from the south; on 15 July, either through some fault of the helm or a strong current, we were carried six points off course. On 16 July we again encountered ice and for two days after that the weather was thick and foggy. On 19 July we sighted a high point of land many of us recognized:

Mount Raleigh which stands in 66° 37′ north latitude. This occurred at one of the clock in the afternoon while we were on a southerly course. By midnight of that same day we were athwart the strait we had discovered and gone up on Captain Davis' first voyage. Despite the wind's being somewhat against us, we again entered the strait and sailed up it for as many as three score leagues so that, at about two of the clock in the afternoon of 23 July, we anchored amid the isles at the bottom of the strait. These isles we named the Earl of Cumberland Isles, which was something our captain had previously neglected to do.

While riding at anchor among those isles, a great whale passed close by our ship and continued to the westward. The compass variation there was 30° to the westward. We departed that same evening, shaping our course back to sea; two days later we had reached the mouth of the strait but lay becalmed. The weather at that time was very hot. Master Bruton, for pastime, took some mariners and went onto an island where we could see some dogs running about. On that island they came upon the graves of many of the people. Too, they found where much train [seal or whale] oil had been spilled on the ground. They also saw, close-up, the dogs we had seen from the ship. The animals were so well fed and fat they scarce could run.

On 26 July there was a storm and a gale from the southwest, but it was of short duration so that by the morn of 27 July we could set our course southward, with the result that at noon of 29 July a sighting on the sun told us we were in latitude 62°. On 30 July we coasted a great bank of ice which lay athwart the entrance to a wide gulf, or inlet, lying between latitudes 62° and 63°. This inlet we called Lumley's Inlet. As we sailed along the coasts there, we ofttimes noticed that there are such violent currents that in places the waters whirl and sound very much as they might when rushing down a rapids or going beneath a narrow bridge.

On the last day of the month we sailed by a foreland which we named Warwick's Foreland. It was in the vicinity of that foreland that we fell into the grip of a very strong current. There was at the time a fresh gale blowing and we had all of our sails out. But it also happened that an ice island lay between us and the land. We became greatly perplexed when, despite our bulging sails, we did not appear to be moving, at least in relation to the island of ice.

We then thought to take bearings on certain landmarks ashore. When we did that, we quickly learned that, instead of standing still, we were going very fast—yet the ice was being carried even faster by the current. Our speed was such we soon had Warwick's Foreland well astern of us, and we found ourselves traversing the mouth of a great gulf where the waters whirled and roared and behaved as though a great tide from the east was being met by one equally as great from the west.

On 1 August we were still on a southerly course and coasting a bank of ice which was being driven by the winds, or carried by the currents, out of the great gulf, when we fell in with a cape which stands in 61° 10′. We named it Cape Chidley, and for various days following our sighting it we coasted the land which trends toward the south. The weather during that time was variable with fogs and calms, brisk winds and gales, though it would be truthful to say the gales were little ones insofar as none lasted for more than hours. On 12 August we approached an island to which we gave the name of Darcy's Island. On it we spied three deer. Hoping to take one, or all of them, for their meat, we put off in our boat and landed. But the deer were very wary. Twice we pursued them clear around the isle without our getting close enough for a shot. Then they foiled us completely by leaping into the sea and swimming toward some other islands which lay about three leagues off. We did not attempt to follow them as our boat was so small it would not have accommodated one of the animals even had we been able to overtake them, for each of them was as big as a fair-sized cow. Too, they were such fast swimmers I believe they would have outdistanced us anyway. For all of our trouble, we returned aboard with a single hare, one I managed to shoot with my piece.

The next day, upon another isle, we saw three or four white bears but our boat was such a poor one we did not even try to land. That same day we struck on a rock while searching for a harbour, causing our vessel to leak so badly we were forced to labour at mending the leak, even though a gale was blowing. This happened on 14 August.

On 15 August we were in almost 52° latitude, and we were greatly concerned about our ships, the *Elizabeth* and the *Sunshine*. Before parting from us, their companies had promised to do their fishing and then wait for us between latitudes 55° and 54°. In order that we might not miss them as we worked southward along the coast, it had been agreed that they would put out markers, beacons, or other tokens upon each headland, island and cape within twenty leagues either way from their fishing grounds. As this had not been done, we had no way of knowing what had become of them; therefore, there appeared to be no purpose in our searching further. Instead, our men were for departing for home at once.

The next day we were blessed with a fair wind from the southwest so we shaped our course for England. The next day, 17 August, we saw many whales. We also saw a ship we judged might be a Biscayan [Portuguese, Spanish or Basque from the Bay of Biscay] whaler.

We arrived in Dartmouth, giving thanks to God, on 15 September 1587.

It is not difficult to trace the route taken by Davis on his third and last voyage to the northwest. Not only have we Janes' account of the voyage, but we have Davis' *Traverse Book* which gives us such items as the courses set, the wind and weather conditions, and the elevations of the Pole in degrees and minutes.

Upon leaving England, Davis and his men sailed directly to the southern tip of Greenland. Rounding Cape Farewell, they passed northward up the coast to latitude 64° where, says Davis in his *Traverse Book*, "We came to anchor among low islands which lay before the high land"—Gilbert's Sound. It was there they parted from the *Elizabeth* and the *Sunshine*. Their arrival there was on 16 June; they departed 21 June.

On 30 June Davis gives us their latitude: 72° 12′. He also has this entry in his book, "Since the 21 of this month I have continually coasted the shore of Greenland." This was the farthest north Davis sailed. On 1 July his course was west-southwest. Janes says they sailed for forty or more leagues; Davis gives the figure of forty-four leagues. In either event, they were in latitude 71° 40′. That was when they fell in with the great bank of ice. At the time they would have been about 5°, or close to 350 miles, north of Mount Raleigh, which stands in 66° 37′, and well to the westward of Cape Dyer, due to the fact that the longitudinal lines narrow the farther north one goes.

Winds from the north forced them to turn southward so that on 19 July they sighted Mount Raleigh; on 23 July they were at the extreme end of the cul-de-sac which is Cumberland Sound (on Baffin Island). Coming out of Cumberland Sound, they sailed southward, passing the mouth of Frobisher Bay on 30 July. Unaware that Frobisher had been before them, they named the bay Lumley Inlet. Farther south they sighted Resolution Island, which Davis called Warwick Foreland; thence they sailed across the mouth of Hudson Strait to Cape Chidley and then down the Labrador coast to latitude 52°. That was when they shaped course for home.

Davis' account of the voyage and Janes' vary in minor ways. For instance, there is a slight discrepancy in the account of the two ships wanting to give up the venture and go fishing. Although Davis says it had been understood, from the beginning, that the *Elizabeth* and the *Sunshine* should go fishing, according to Janes' account when the ships wanted to go southward from the vicinity of Cape Farewell, Davis threatened them with dire consequences unless they continued on to latitude 64°. In addition, Janes makes no mention that the Biscayan whaler might have had piratical intentions: Davis says the Biscayan chased them.

PART TWO

Voyages to the South Atlantic

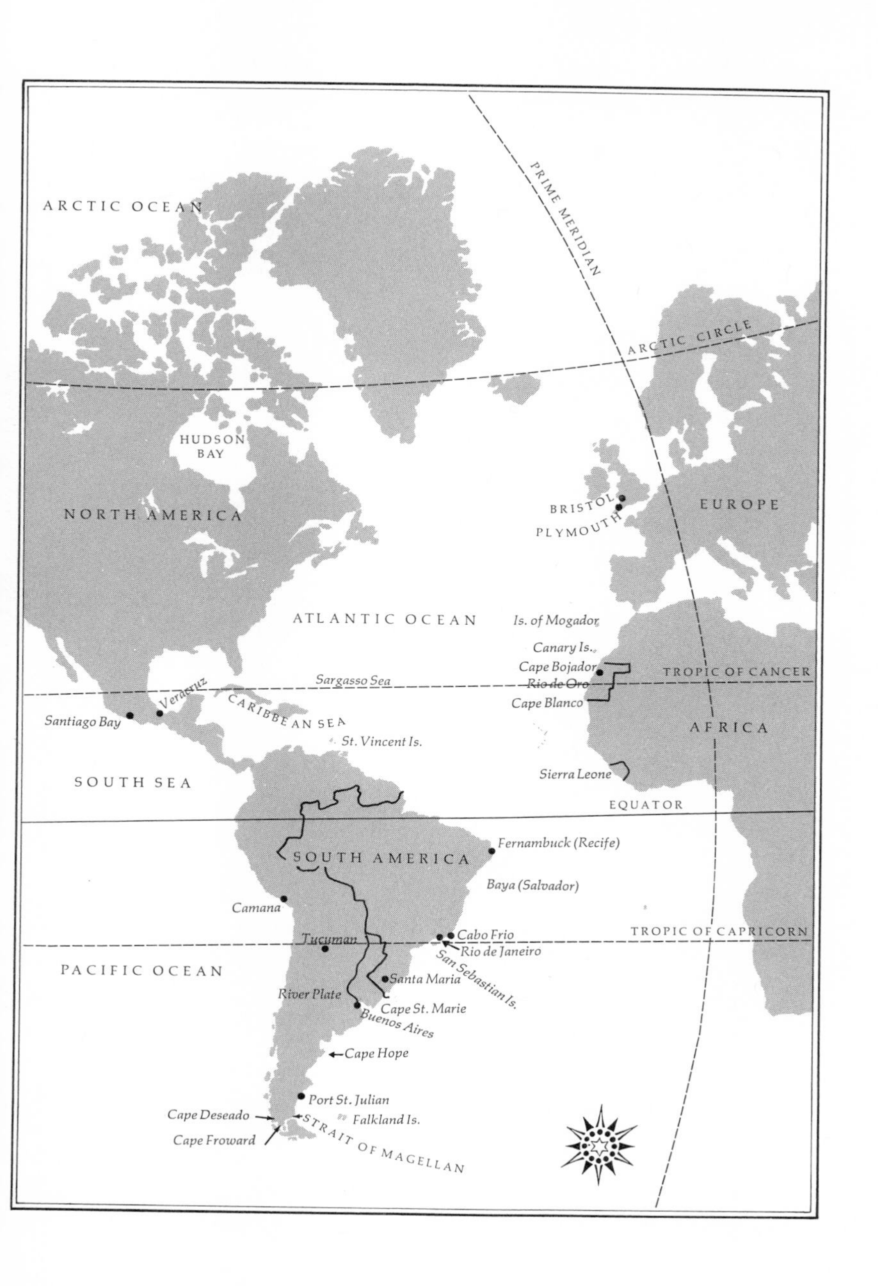
ARCTIC OCEAN
PRIME MERIDIAN
ARCTIC CIRCLE
HUDSON BAY
NORTH AMERICA
BRISTOL
PLYMOUTH
EUROPE
ATLANTIC OCEAN
Is. of Mogador
Canary Is.
Cape Bojador
TROPIC OF CANCER
Sargasso Sea
Rio de Oro
Cape Blanco
Veracruz
CARIBBEAN SEA
Santiago Bay
AFRICA
St. Vincent Is.
SOUTH SEA
Sierra Leone
EQUATOR
Fernambuck (Recife)
SOUTH AMERICA
Baya (Salvador)
Camana
Cabo Frio
TROPIC OF CAPRICORN
Tucuman
Rio de Janeiro
PACIFIC OCEAN
Santa Maria
San Sebastian Is.
River Plate
Cape St. Marie
Buenos Aires
Cape Hope
Port St. Julian
Cape Deseado
Falkland Is.
Cape Froward
STRAIT OF MAGELLAN

The voyage of

John Winter

as told by Edward Cliffe

In Elizabethan England there were three large, wealthy, and powerful families, the Winters, the Hawkinses, and the Fenners, who had taken to the sea on both a commercial and a privateering basis. Sir Francis Drake, a kinsman of the Hawkins family, was a member of the Hawkins group. All three families were conducting private wars against the Spaniards. For example, John Hawkins and Francis Drake made a privateering voyage into the West Indies in 1576 where they met with a disastrous setback at St. Juan de Ulna (Vera Cruz). Very shortly thereafter the Winter family staged a much more successful raid into the Caribbean. There were also rivalries between the family groups, despite their common objective. Sometimes, though, they collaborated.

Collaboration was probably the case when Captain John Winter sailed with Drake on Drake's famous round-the-world voyage of 1577-79. The fact that Winter was in command of one of Drake's largest ships, the *Elizabeth,* suggests the Winter family may have had a financial stake in the venture. It also indicates the policy of the English Government toward piracy: John Winter's uncle, Sir William Winter, was a member of the Admiralty Board.

Drake obviously had great faith in Captain John Winter. When it was decided that Thomas Doughty, a gentleman on the voyage, should be tried for treason at Port St. Julian, prior to the expedition's entering the

Strait of Magellan, Drake appointed Winter to head the jury. It was a task, says one historian, that Captain Winter did not relish. Later, when Doughty had been sentenced to die, Winter pleaded with Drake to spare him. He even said he would keep Doughty in his custody, and guarantee that he would commit no more mischief. His offer was refused and Doughty was executed.

Edward Cliffe, the author of this account, was a mariner on the *Elizabeth*.

On 19 September, 1577, there went out of the Thames a good and new ship called the *Elizabeth* which was of the burden of eighty tons. In consort with her was a pinnace of twelve tons named the *Benedict*. The said *Elizabeth* and her pinnace arrived, after certain days, in Plymouth. There and awaiting their coming lay three more goodly ships: the *Pelican* of 100 tons; the bark, *Marigold*, of thirty tons, and a flyboat of fifty tons. The *Pelican* was the admiral ship of this fleet of five vessels which had in them persons to the number of 164 and which were victualled and furnished for a voyage into the South Sea. It was intended the voyage begin on 15 September so on that date we hoist sail. But before we could clear Land's End, contrary winds—they were in all truth tempests—forced us to seek shelter in Falmouth. During these tempests our ships were so hurt we deemed it necessary to return to Plymouth to repair the damage. It was, therefore, 13 December before we could again proceed with the voyage.

This time, our fortunes were better. On 25 December we raised Cape Cantin which lies in 32° 30′ of north latitude on the Barbary [Morocco] coast of Africa, and near to a town called Asaphi. Sailing south-southwestward along this coast, which is very high and mountainous, for about eighteen leagues we came to the Island of Mogador. Mogador is about a mile in circumference, lies an English mile from the mainland and has no people. We lay off this isle for the time it took one of our boats to take soundings and search for a suitable harbour. The quest was successful as the boat's crew discovered a safe haven with five fathoms of water and well sheltered by a high point of rock. Into this haven we brought the fleet on 27 December.

No sooner were our ships at anchor than the people of the country, whom we knew to be Moors, came down to the shore of the mainland and stood watching us, whereupon our general, Sir Francis Drake, caused a white flag to be waved continuously at them as a token we meant them no harm. It also happened we had in our company a man who had once been a captive of the Moors and therefore knew some of their language. This prompted our general to send this man, along with others, ashore in a boat. The boat having arrived by where the Moors were, the man leaped ashore and came to no harm. He talked to the Moors and they expressed their friendship for us, both in words and by signs. An arrangement was made whereby he would remain ashore while two of their people would return, with the boat, to the ships. These two Moors received gifts from the hand of our general, after which they were returned to the land and our man came back to us. Not without reason, we fully believed we had established the most friendly relations with these people.

The next morning, a number of Moors again appeared on the shore of the mainland. This time, they had a number of camels with them. As the camels had on their backs what appeared to be items of merchandise, we were convinced they wished to traffic with us. Our general sent a boat ashore to inquire as to what they had brought. But he was careful to warn the men to remain in their boat and not allow themselves to be lured ashore. This warning one of our men chose to ignore, for no sooner had the boat neared the shore than he did a hasty, and foolish, thing. He leaped ashore. The Moors immediately seized him, placed him on a horse, and carried him off. We saw him no more.

In the meantime, we were not devoting all of our attention to the Moors. On the island various of our men were busily engaged in fitting together a pinnace, one of four which had been brought, in pieces, from England. On 31 December, our pinnace having been completed, we left the Island of Mogador. But scarce were we out of our sheltered harbour than we were met by such strong and contrary winds that we were forced to beat back and forth until 4 January. Then the wind became favourable, coming out of the northeast so we could go before it on a south-southwest course, which course we held until 7 January, when we came by Cape de Guer in 30° north of the Equator. Near that cape our newly built pinnace took three Spanish fishing boats which are called cantars. From thence, and taking the cantars with us, we ran southwest and south-southwest until 10 January, upon which date we discovered ourselves to be in 27° 4′ of latitude and ten leagues south-southwest from Cape Bojador on the mainland of Africa. From there, we ran south by west until noon of 13 January when we had sight of Rio de Oro, where our pinnace captured a Portuguese caravel. Two days later the *Marigold* took another caravel, this one near Cape de las Barbas. We continued along the coast, which is low and sandy there, until we arrived at Cape Blanco which lies in 20° 30′ of north latitude. Seen from the northward, Cape Blanco looks not unlike the corner of a high wall standing upright out of the water.

It was there we caught our first sight of the Southern Cross, raised 9° 30′. The Southern Cross is a group of four stars 30° north of the South Pole. A sighting on it should be taken on the lowest star. If such a sighting gives you 30° then you are directly on the Equator. By then you shall have entirely lost sight of Polaris [the North Star] which stands at 0° of the North Pole.

Off Cape Blanco we took a ship, with but two men in her, the remainder of her crew having fled. We still had this ship with us when we entered a haven about five leagues within the shelter of the cape. There we cleaned and trimmed our ships and when we put out to sea again on 22 January we left the Spaniards and their cantars too, excepting for one. That particular cantar we exchanged for our twelve-ton pinnace, the *Benedict*. The course we set was to the southwest, which meant we had the wind continually at our backs as northeasterly winds are common there. Our progress was such that on 26 January we found ourselves in 15° 15′ north latitude. While on that course we sighted and ran by the Island of Bonavista, and on 27 January at three of the clock in the afternoon we were approaching the Island of Mayo, which is high and hilly, save for its northern part. That part of it is very low and stretches out into the sea for as much as a league. We came to anchor under the western shore of Mayo on 28 January and remained there for two days.

During those two days, our general appointed Masters John Winter and Thomas Doughty as the commanders of a company of seventy men charged with traversing the island from west to east in a search for fresh victuals. As we were marching across the island we came upon a house which had a garden. The garden had grapes and other things growing in it such as one might expect to find thriving in an English garden in summer—even though the month was January. In our march we also came to trees which bear a fruit called coconuts. These coconuts are of the size of a man's head and have a thick, brownish-coloured outer coat, or shell. But immediately within that outer shell is a layer of whitish meat and within the layer of meat is a liquid, both of which are very good. During our passage over the island we saw not a single inhabitant. Warned, no doubt, of our coming, they had fled. We did, though, see living things: goats, many of them, running wild. They proved so wary we managed to take only a few of the youngest kids and so, perforce, we returned to the ships all but empty-handed. We were even denied fresh water. The Portuguese had salted the wells.

Since to remain longer on that particular island would have been time wasted, the general ordered all hands back aboard. The anchors were brought in and we departed, setting course for Santiago which lies about ten leagues distant from Mayo. Santiago, to our eyes, seemed a rich and fruitful island. We saw three towns, each close to the shore. However, the people in all of those towns regarded us as enemies. Each of them fired ordnance at us, an act which caused our general, on one occasion, to return the fire but no harm was done either by their shot or ours. Santiago lies in 15° of north latitude and, while ranging along its southern part, we took a Portuguese ship which was laden with wine and other commodities. Having taken this ship, we left Santiago, running south-southwest from it until we were by the Island of Fogo [the Burning Isle]. Fogo acquired its name because it has one high, volcanic mountain which continuously casts out flame and smoke. Two leagues to the westward of Fogo is the island of Brava. At Brava we would have anchored in order to take in fresh water, but the sea was so deep our anchors would not hold.

As we lay off Brava, our general discharged all of the Portuguese prisoners—with the exception of one. That one was a pilot whose name was Nuno da Silva. All of the others he placed in the pinnace we had fitted together at Mogador and let them go free, after giving them sufficient water and victuals to see them safely to land.

The date we sent them from us was 1 February. The following day we set course from Brava and ran south-southwest until 9 February. On that date we were within 4° of the Equator. At the time, though we lay becalmed for most part, there were storms of thunder and lightning and much rain fell, which was good.

On 17 February we were on the Equator. The heat was so great we sweated enormously and, in all truth, it was as though we were by a roaring fireplace or in a hothouse. While on or near the Equator we saw many strange and interesting fishes. Flying fish were in abundance and sometimes, when they were being pursued by dolphins, various of them would fall onto the decks. From 17 February we held course toward the south-southwest. This we continued to do until 5 April, upon which date we had a very sweet smell from the land. At noon of that day we took soundings, finding the sea to be two and thirty fathoms in depth with a soft and oozy bottom. Not too long afterwards we again sounded and found that the water had shallowed to eight and twenty fathoms. A sighting on the sun revealed we were in 31° 30′ south. At three of the clock in the afternoon we caught our first sight of the land. Close by the sea it gave the appearance of being a low, flat country; farther inland, though, we could discern high mountains.

We continued our course toward the south-southwest until 14 April which brought us near to a small isle lying in 35° south and by Cape St. Marie in the entrance to the River Plate. From the isle we ran along the coast of the mainland for as many as seven or eight leagues, finally coming to anchor under a headland which our general called Cape Joy. There we took in fresh water. Having watered, we departed and sailed, by our reckoning, another fifteen leagues to the west-southwest and this brought us into a deep bay. In the bottom of this bay there is a large rock, rising high out of the water and lying not far from the mainland. Between the rock and the land there is a well-sheltered road. Into that road we brought our fleet, remaining there until the following day while we employed ourselves killing seals, which were plentiful, for their meat.

From that particular road we ran about twenty leagues and again took in fresh water as we were still in the mouth of the River Plate. Resuming course, on 27 April we came to the southern side of the entrance to the river. There, we found the water to be very shallow for as many as three or four leagues out into the sea. That night we became separated from our flyboat.

Upon departing from the River Plate we held to the southwest, keeping the land to starboard of us, the while we were thwarted by contrary winds and foul weather. On 12 May we were in 47° and, at ten of the clock in the morning, we sighted a high headland which our general named Cape Hope. Coming, in the late afternoon, up by this cape, we anchored about a league offshore from it and there we spent the night. In the morning the general crewed a boat and went to the land. By doing so, we came very near to losing him, for we were visited by a sudden spell of thick weather accompanied by a stiff gale from the southwest. The *Marigold,* not without great risk, weighed her anchor and ran in to the shore. By her action the general and his men were found and taken aboard. That done, the *Marigold* anchored under the shore where she was somewhat sheltered. Meanwhile, the other ships became so endangered by the gale that they brought in their anchors and ran out to sea.

The next morning, 14 May, our flyboat which had been missing since 27 April appeared and joined the *Marigold.* Later that same morning the general and various men went ashore in their boat where they saw two men of the country, which men were naked except for a single garment of skin each wore wrapped about his head and shoulders. To these inhabitants of the land our general waved a white cloth and made other friendly gestures. However, they remained somewhat wary. They refused to come near to the general but remained at a distance and tried conversing in words no one could understand. Finally, they left. The following day, though, the general returned to the same spot, hoping the men would again appear. They did not. But they had come and gone, leaving lying on the ground a sizable heap of freshly slain fowls, including some ostriches. Besides the birds there was a small bag containing coloured stones. In the belief the people had intended the fowls and the stones as gifts, the general and his men took them and returned aboard. The anchors were then weighed and the *Marigold,* accompanied by the flyboat, put out to sea and rejoined the other ships—excepting the prize [the *Maria*]. During foul weather the prize had become separated from the other ships and was still missing.

On 16 May we ran into a bay southward of Cape Hope, cast our anchors and lay there overnight. In the morning, the general sent the *Elizabeth* southward in search of the missing prize. He, in his own ship, went northward for the same purpose. Meanwhile, the *Marigold* and the cantar were under instructions to further explore the bay in the hope of finding a better anchorage. On the morning of 18 May the *Marigold* and the cantar put out to sea in order to rejoin the fleet and inform the general they had located a good road. Upon hearing this, the general accompanied them back to the safe haven where they lay until the *Elizabeth* returned from her quest to the southward. The prize was still missing. That being so, the *Elizabeth* again put forth on 20 May to continue the search. Unsuccessful, she returned to harbour the following day.

While the ships lay at anchor in that haven, which they did for the space of a fortnight, various things occurred and certain matters received attention. Among the latter, the general decided the flyboat was causing us too much grief so he ordered her run up onto the shore and broken up for firewood. While this was being done, the people of the country became aware of our presence in their land. About thirty of them appeared and seated themselves, in most orderly array, about 100 paces from our men. There they sat, in the form of a circle, with each man clutching his bow but otherwise making no gesture which could be termed unfriendly.

Our general, anxious to establish relations with them, ordered one of our men to go forth, unarmed, and place certain gifts such as mirrors, beads, and other trifles upon the ground. This our man did, and when he had returned to us the people came forward and took the gifts. After that, they came to us in friendship, showing no fear whatsoever. They proved to be a very pleasant people, having but one vice: thievishness. They will steal whatever they can lay hand upon. They even stole the very cap from our general's head because, or so we thought, they could not resist the temptation of its scarlet colouring. From our observation they are a people much given to jollity. They laugh easily and were entranced by the sound of our trumpets and the music of our viols. Too, they were amused beyond belief when Master Winter danced for them. They are a people of middle stature, well made, and brown-skinned. Some of them paint their faces in divers colours;

their clothing is made entirely from the skins of beasts while upon their heads they wear a certain kind of cap, or hat, with ends which hang down over their shoulders. As for food, they eat at least some of their meat uncooked. This we learned by finding bones they had picked and gnawed but which still had shreds of raw flesh clinging to them.

Seals are plentiful in that bay. Once upon a little isle we slew 200 of them within an hour.

On 3 June we departed from there and when we were off Cape Hope we divested ourselves of the cantar for the same reason we had rid ourselves of the flyboat. But the cantar we did not break up. We just emptied her and then set her adrift. On 19 June we met up with the prize which had been missing since 13 May. The next day, 20 June, we came to harbour in a bay which lies in 49° 30′. This is the place where Magellan wintered and it is called Port St. Julian. We quickly knew it to be the same place for, upon the land, we found a gibbet. By that gibbet were the bones of men, executed by Magellan for having conspired against him.

On 22 June our general, having gone onto the mainland with seven or eight men, met three people of the country who are known as Patagons [Patagonians]. The three Patagons approached our men, the while they made signs that the general and his company should go to their boat and depart. At that, one of the gentlemen had a mind to impress the Patagons with the power of his English bow. He made to shoot an arrow. But even though he did not aim it at any of them, the Patagons mistook his purpose and thought he meant them harm. The gentleman had the further misfortune in that, when he drew, his bowstring broke, thus leaving him without a weapon. By then, the Patagons were letting fly arrows at our men. The gentleman who had started it all was struck and so grievously wounded he died two days later. The master gunner, who was also one of the general's company, was killed as he was trying to level his caliver at the Patagons. The arrow which slew him struck him in the chest with such force a portion of it protruded from his back. The general and the remainder of his men retreated to their boat and escaped. Later, they returned for the body of the slain man. The people of the country had stripped the corpse of its clothing and, for reasons known only to themselves, had thrust an English arrow into one of its eyes.

The Spaniards have long reported that these Patagons are giants. From our observations that tale is but another of their notorious lies, for we saw none of unusually large stature. Indeed I have seen men here in England who are taller than their tallest.

On 30 June Master Thomas Doughty was brought to trial, after having been accused of certain offences. Upon his being found guilty, he was condemned by Master Drake. On 2 July 1578 he was beheaded and lies buried beside the two men slain by the Patagons.

We remained in Port St. Julian for two months, during which time we had weather such as is common here in England in the depth of winter, or probably a trifle colder. During our stay there we trimmed our ships, repaired them as best we could, and took on supplies both of wood and fresh water. We departed on 17 August at about noon. On the third day after that, we were standing by the Strait of Magellan which is named for its discoverer. It lies in 52° 30′ south. In this strait we found no such fierce currents as we had been led to expect, for, in all truth, the ebb and flow is quite ordinary. Five fathoms is the greatest height of tide we experienced. One thing we did notice: The flood from the east stretches so far into the strait it meets the flood from the west, which meeting takes place near the middle of the strait where there is a sharp bend which reminds one of a crooked elbow. To the westward of this most pronounced bend the passage, or strait, trends to the west-northwest, continuing so until the South Sea is reached.

Thirty leagues into the strait, from the eastward, there lie three islands. To the greatest of them our general gave the name Elizabeth, in honour of Her Majesty; to the second isle went the name Bartholomew because we found it on St. Bartholomew's Day. The third isle he called St. George's. St. George's Isle had a numberless store of great fowls which cannot fly because their wings are so small they are of use only for swimming. In colour these birds are black on the back, while their underparts are speckled black and white. They do not even walk as do other fowls. Instead, they stand upright on their short legs so that, seen from afar, they might well be mistaken for little children. Their flesh, when it is cooked, is similar in taste to that of a fat English goose. For their meat, we took many of them simply by hitting them on their heads with staves, their only protection whatsoever being that they had shallow holes into which they could go. These holes did not save them. We attached hooks to our staves and dragged them forth. One man would pull a bird out; a second man stood ready to slay it. They durst not, while alive, be touched by hand; their crooked beaks are dangerous.

The land within the strait is, for the most part, very high and the monstrous hills have snow upon them during the months of August, September, and October, the months when we saw them. But notwithstanding the snow on the upper parts of these high hills, their lower parts are well-wooded with evergreen trees. We passed out of this strait on 6 September and, once in the South Sea, we ran to the northwest for as many as seventy leagues. Then the wind turned against us, becoming so violent and bringing with it so much rain and snow, and thick fogs, that for the space of three whole weeks we never hoist a sail. We were driven so far to the southward that on one occasion we were in 57° south of the Equator.

On 15 September there was an eclipse of the moon which began just after the setting of the sun, at about six of the clock as we were then at the time of the vernal equinox. This same eclipse, according to our sea calendar, was occurring in England before one of the clock on the morning of 16 September. This six hour difference told us we were one-quarter way around the world, westward from the meridian of London, England.

On 30 September there was a very foul night with the seas so monstrous that during the darkness we became separated from the *Marigold*. As she was never again seen, we judged her lost. The weather continuing to be vile, a week later, on 7 October, the general's ships were forced to seek shelter among the islands along the shore to the eastward, coming to anchor in a dangerous bay which had many rocks. That night we lost company with Master Drake's ship. The following day, by exercising the greatest of care, we escaped the rocks and worked our way into more open and safer waters. As there was still no sign of the general's ship, we put into the mouth of the strait, coming to anchor in an open bay. It was our belief the other ship would come searching for us and, of course, find us. For two successive nights we also lighted great fires upon the shore, hoping they would act as beacons and guide the general to us.

But when the general did not appear, we went farther into the strait and anchored in a sound. There we lay for three weeks. We named the sound Port of Good Health and for the very good reason that during our sojourn there our men regained, in wonderful fashion, their health. Upon our coming into the sound most all of them had been sick from the wet, the cold, and the evil diet. At Port of Good Health, the land provided us with fresh victuals, including giant mussels, some measuring twenty inches in length, whose flesh was pleasant eating.

We left there on 1 November and, instead of returning to the South Sea, the voyage was given over. This was by Master Winter's command. He despaired of ever seeing Master Drake again. He also expressed, in words, his doubts the winds would ever allow us to reach Peru. And so it was that, much against the will of the mariners, we started back through the strait. When we arrived by St. George's Island we slew and took aboard a great store of the aforementioned fowls. That done, we departed, passing out of the strait on 11 November, after which we directed our course to the northeast until the end of the month. By then we were again in the mouth of the River Plate and by an island we had touched upon before, one which had upon it an infinite number of seals. Some of these seals were of an incredible size, measuring up to sixteen feet in length. Totally unaccustomed to man, they were without fear of us. Indeed we had to club them out of our way when we set about fitting together a pinnace, a task which took several days.

When our pinnace was completed, we left the isle and went to another one where fresh water was available. There we filled our pipes [water casks] and, that done, we departed from the River Plate on 1 January 1579. Shaping a northerly course until 20 January we found ourselves to be in 24°, or very near the Tropic of Capricorn, and off a certain Portuguese town on the coast of Brazil. The name of this town is St. Vincent, and it was there we lost our pinnace and eight men due to foul weather. The truth is, we came very near to losing our ship as well when the wind, uniting with a strong current, carried us perilously near the rocks. We escaped that danger and, having succeeded in working our ship farther off-shore and into more open water, we risked anchoring in the hope we could ride out the worst of the weather.

But the strain upon our cable was too great. It broke and we lost an anchor. In attempting to let go a second anchor, misfortune befell us. Due the heaving motion of the ship the capstan got the better of the seamen. Wrenched from their hands, the bars spun violently about, knocking the brains out of one man, breaking the legs of another, and sorely injuring various others. Escaping from that predicament, we gave over the idea of anchoring. Instead, we put out sail and ran to sea, finally coming to a place called Tanay where we sought for, and found, shelter in a road under an island. That same island treated us kindly in other ways: It provided us with both wood and water.

While we were lying in the road, a canoe bearing three Portuguese came out to us. Curiosity had brought them. They wanted to find out what ship we were and from what country we had come. When our captain replied, saying we were Englishmen and that we came in peace and wished only to trade, they marvelled greatly. Never, they said, had they ever before been visited by an English ship. It was arranged that one of the Portuguese would remain with us while one of our men went ashore to speak with the governor of the town. The exchange having taken place, before too long a canoe, a very large one, came out to us. The canoe had a single Portuguese in it but he was not alone; besides him there were a number of men of the country—all of them completely naked. We trafficked with them and obtained two small oxen, a young hog, a number of hens, as well as certain fruits, including lemons and oranges. In return, we gave them linen, combs, knives, and other trifles.

However, the canoe was still with us when a second one arrived. This one brought no trade goods. Instead, it had a message from the governor. The governor said he was forbidding his people to trade with us unless we brought our ship into the harbour and close to the town. This our captain was not of a mind to do as he was mistrustful of the Portuguese. Nevertheless, we did take our ship nearer the town, thus making it appear we did intend to enter the harbour itself. But once we had our man safely back with us we departed and went to the nearby island of St. Sebastion. There we did some fishing. That night a Brazilian slave of the Portuguese, at no small risk to himself, came to us. By signs, the man told us the Portuguese planned to take us by surprise and capture both us and our ship. Forewarned, we readied ourselves and, come morning, the Portuguese did appear in several large canoes, some having as many as forty men in them. But when they saw we were prepared for them, they did not attempt to carry out their treacherous purpose. That night, though, two of our men stole our boat and deserted to the Portuguese.

We left there on 17 March and, continuing northward, crossed the Equator on 13 April. Six days later, on 19 April, we had our first sight of Polaris. From 1 May until 5 May, being by then under the Tropic of Cancer, we had the marvellous experience of having to sail, for as many as 100 leagues, through what is sometimes called the Sea of Weeds [Sargasso Sea]. From thence, we held our course toward the northeast until we were in 47°. On 22 May we ran east-northeast so that by 29 May we were in 51°. The following day we came in sight of St. Ives [in Cornwall]. On 2 June we came to anchor in Ilfracombe in Devonshire.

Thus, and after manifold troubles and dangers, and having passed into the South Sea by way of the Strait of Magellan, and having passed back through that same strait, it pleased God to bring us safely into our own country.

Edward Cliffe does his captain an injustice by placing on him the sole responsibility for giving up the voyage. Everywhere Winter was scathingly described as being the owner of feet as cold as his name. Upon his arrival back in England, with his account of what had taken place in and near the Strait of Magellan, it was generally accepted that Drake had perished. When Sir Francis turned up very much alive, Winter was promptly branded a deserter. According to the historian George Wychirley, Winter was tried, condemned, and sentenced to be hanged, but Drake intervened and had him set free.

Winter had, it is true, allowed at least a part of his crew to persuade him he should turn back, but in most ways he had behaved as a good captain should. Neither his ship nor his men were in condition to continue. Drake could understand, better than most, Winter's action.

Although he was not the pilot of the *Elizabeth,* Cliffe gives its latitudes. He probably got the latitudinal readings from other accounts of the voyage. (Cliffe did not write his account of the voyage until several years after the voyage.) His mention of the eclipse of the moon is particularly interesting. Sixteenth-century navigators, lacking chronometers, welcomed eclipses as the one sure way of ascertaining their true longitude. Cliffe states that this particular eclipse indicated that they were one-quarter of the way around the world from the Prime Meridian. This seems highly doubtful. They could not, at the very most, have been more than 75° westward from the meridian of London.

In one respect Cliffe's facts re the eclipse are reasonably accurate. He states it occurred at the time of the vernal equinox—on September 15, just after the setting of the sun, at about six of the clock. Actually, as they were using the Old Style Calendar, they would have been past the equinox by about five days. The sun would have gone down very shortly after six o'clock.

The voyage of some ships sent out by

The Earl of Cumberland

as told by John Sarracoll

The Earl of Cumberland, fourteenth Baron Clifford of Westmoreland, and hereditary sheriff of County Westmoreland, was a remarkable man. Today, the earl is relatively unknown, but in his time, he was one of England's most colourful figures. Born George Clifford in his father's castle at Brougham in 1558, he had the advantage of wealth and an illustrious family name.

Educated at Oxford and Cambridge, he became so skilled at the sport of tilting that he was, write historians, "always the Queen's champion" at tournaments. Queen Elizabeth gave him a peerage and made him a Knight of the Garter.

In the 1580's he became interested, partly from patriotism and partly for profit, in outfitting ventures such as the one described in the narrative.

John Sarracoll was the Earl of Cumberland's personal representative on the voyage. When he wrote this account he was probably reporting to the earl.

On 26 June 1586 we departed from Gravesend in two ships, our admiral, the *Red Dragon* of 260 tons, commanded by Master Robert Withrington, and the bark *Clifford* of 130 tons, our vice-admiral which had for its captain Master Christopher Lister. The *Red Dragon*'s company consisted of 130 men; that of the *Clifford* 70 men. John Anthony was the master of the *Red Dragon*, while his brother, William, was master of the *Clifford*.

Both these tall ships had been furnished and outfitted at the expense of the Earl of Cumberland.

On 24 July we came into Plymouth where we were detained by westerly winds until 17 August and, while lying there, we were joined by two more ships, thus completing our fleet of four. One of these ships, which henceforth would be our rear admiral, was called the *Roe* and was captained by Master Hawes. The other was a very fine pinnace, the *Dorothy*, belonging to Sir Walter Raleigh.

On 20 August we were at sea, but still quite near to Plymouth, when we met a fleet of sixteen hulks [merchantmen], all heavily laden. We hailed these ships, demanding to know who they were. They replied they were of Hamburg and had come from Lisbon. Upon hearing this our admiral, though in a most courteous manner, demanded that their admiral strike his sails, and to send people aboard, so that news might be exchanged. Their admiral refused to come aboard or to strike his sails, though he did take in his flag. The vice-admiral of the hulks, being in the lead at the time, would strike neither his flag nor his sails but, instead, he held on course without budging in any way. At that, our admiral lent him a shot. The shot having been returned double, there grew up a small quarrel. While shots were being traded, one of the hulks became afraid and struck amain, taking in both sails and flag and thereby submitting.

This ship was laid aboard but how many of our men were sent into her I do not know. At the time, we were giving chase to the hulk which was the farthest downwind, reasoning that our admiral was determined to make all of them strike. However, the weather thickened with both fog and rain so we gave up the chase. It was morning before our fleet was reunited and it was then we learned that Captain Hawes in the *Roe* had boarded a hulk, but had taken only a few victuals out of her before letting her go. From the hulk's company it was learned that seven other ships had left Lisbon with them. Those seven, though, had been so richly laden they had not dared enter the [English] Channel. Instead, they had chosen to sail clear around Ireland and Scotland in order to avoid being taken by such as we.

The next day, late in the evening, we sighted five more sail to the eastward of us. Though night was near at hand, we managed to get close enough to the largest of these hulks to hail it. Its company said all of the ships were of Hamburg. However, and right away, another of them hailed us and said they were of Denmark. We considered boarding one or more of these ships but our admiral, by making use of a piece of his ordnance, as well as a trumpet, ordered us to desist. He was more desirous of our keeping on course at that time than he was of anything else.

On 22 August a strong westerly gale drove us back to the eastward, finally forcing us to seek shelter in Dartmouth. There we lay for seven days, waiting more favourable weather. On 29 August we came out again to truly begin our voyage, with the winds treating us so kindly that we rounded Spain and fell in with Barbary coast on 17 September. On 18 September we were in the road of Santa Cruz in the Canaries [Canary Islands]. Three days later we raised the Island of Feurtaventura, which is also one of the Canaries. While running along the coast of this island we spied three men, standing atop a hill close by the sea, waving a white flag at us. Curious to know why they were doing this, two boats were manned and sent in. The three men proved to be no more than ragged knaves; their news was that, in August, Lanzarote [another of the Canary Islands] had been taken and spoiled by the Turks. As their news was of little interest to us, we proceeded on course, again falling in with the Barbary coast.

On 25 September, at ten of the clock in the morning, we came into the mouth of the Rio de Oro, standing just under the Tropic of Cancer. Its entrance is about two leagues in breadth and we found an anchorage in eight fathoms. The next day our captain took a boat and proceeded upriver for as many as fifteen leagues, discovering that even that far up the river was still broad. He saw no human habitations, no towns, but two poor men came to the shore and talked to the captain. One speaking good Spanish told our captain that, on occasion, French ships called to pick up ox and goat hides but as for other items of trade there were none. We departed from the Rio de Oro on 27 September, and held course to the southward, but very shortly we found ourselves becalmed. On the last day of the month, with the calm still holding, we consulted with our general and it was decided that we should go to Sierra Leone to pick up wood and water for the voyage to the Americas. We would have done this without delay but the calm persisted until 10 October. During those days it was extremely hot and there were many thunderstorms, with a great deal of lightning.

We once more were allowed, by the winds, to get underway so that, on 21 October, we fell in with the coast of Guinea in the height of 8°. We found it to be a very high land, and shortly thereafter we arrived by Sierra Leone. On 23 October, a Sunday, we came to anchor in a bay of fresh water. Going ashore with our boats we met a Portuguese man who told us that if we were intending to take on wood and water we should first visit a nearby town and present the king of the place with gifts of wine and some linen cloth. But our captains did not think it wise we should pay for something we could have for the taking. A number of our men were landed, whereupon the Portuguese, and some Negroes who had appeared, fled into the woods.

We returned to our boats and went and landed in another place, thinking to take a walk in the woods. We had not gone very far when we came, unexpectedly, upon a town of Negroes. Immediately the people saw our men they began to beat on drums and shout. Too, they let fly a hail of arrows. But we were around thirty in number, twenty armed with calivers. We shot off the calivers, causing the Negroes to run away, but we had no way of knowing how many of them were hurt.

We returned to our boats and took on both wood and water without being disturbed in any way. We also caught a considerable store of fish. While we were about our fishing, we also brought up a great, foul monster which was all of nine feet in length. It had a shell a boar spear could not pierce. However, its underbelly was unprotected so we slew it by thrusting swords into it there. As we were doing this, the creature got hold of a sword with its mouth and bent it. When it was finally dead we slit its belly, and found it contained little else but pebbles, none of any value.

On 4 November we went on shore and to a town of the Negroes which stood about a saker [small cannon] shot inland from the southeast shore of the bay where our ships were then lying. The town had about 200 newly built houses, which were surrounded by a high, strong wall made from the trunks of large trees. These tree trunks were so well and closely fitted together they would have defied a rat's getting through them. But it so chanced we came upon a port, or gate, in the wall which had been left open.

Too, fortune also favoured us in that we took the inhabitants completely by surprise. Seizing the advantage offered us, we rushed through the port with such noise and fierceness that the people fled in terror into the nearby forest. After examining the town, and expressing our admiration at its cleanliness, we set fire to it. As the roofs of the dwellings were of straw and reeds, the whole place burned within minutes.

In cleared spaces surrounding the walls of their town, the Negroes grew rice, which rice was then in stacks not yet threshed. Our men threshed it for them. They beat out as much as fifteen tons of it and brought all of it aboard. On other journeys into the woods near our anchorage, we came upon various places where the people had driven stakes into the ground and set up images upon them. Before these images were placed offerings of eggs, meat, rice, and even round stones. From this custom of theirs we concluded they must be a most barbarous people. During our stay there a good part of our men were smitten with a violent sickness in their bellies, which sickness, thanks to God, did not last long and the men all recovered.

We departed Sierra Leone on 17 November, setting our course for the Americas and, of course, the Strait of Magellan.

As we began immediately to drop southward toward the Equator, we fully expected the weather to become hotter. Instead, we were again fortunate in that winds and rain made the heat bearable. But we were not without troubles. On 24 November divers of our men became sick with the calenture, a fever one may contract in the tropical regions. It can cause men to become delirious and even to leap overboard. Two seamen died of the disorder. The remainder, for which we gave thanks to God, recovered. On 2 January, at which time we were in the height of 28° south, we caught our first sight of the main of the Americas. Two days later, while standing in 30° 20′, we found ourselves about six leagues to eastward of a high coast, though to southward we could discern that the land was becoming flat and low. We took soundings, finding the water to be sixteen fathoms, and the bottom sandy. As we were low on drinking water we would have gone on shore to replenish our supply but, being unable to see anything resembling a decent harbour, we put farther out to sea and continued on a southerly course.

There is one thing here which I feel merits mention and it is this: From Christmas, which we celebrated in goodly fashion but within the limit of our means, until well on into the month of January we had been, at all times, close to the Equator. Yet we had not suffered from the heat. We had the winds to thank. The winds had been both constant and variable and, in all, of such a nature that there were occasions when a woolen gown would have been welcomed.

On 10 January, and when we were about eight leagues offshore and just to the northward of the mouth of the River Plate, it was my good fortune to sight a sail. We gave chase and, coming up with her at about three of the clock in the afternoon, we took her, finding her to be of fifty tons burden. To our great surprise, her master was an Englishman named Cocke who had been born in Lee. Besides Master Cocke and the other crew members, this ship had as passengers two Portuguese women and a child. There were other passengers as well, unwilling ones. Negro slaves. There were forty-five of these black men and we were told that each of them, when sold, would bring 400 ducats. Besides people, this ship had considerable merchandise in the form of rice, sugar, marmalade, and fruits preserved in sugar syrup.

Because the master of the ship was English, and we could converse with him easily, we examined him at length. By doing so, we learned a great deal about the country and its various settlements. He told us that along the River Plate there are five towns, some having as many as seventy and more houses. The town nearest the mouth of the river, about fifty leagues up it, is called Buenos Aires. The farthest upriver town—in Cocke's estimation it is fully 230 leagues inland—is called Tucaman. All of these five towns depend very largely upon what the surrounding country produces, namely cattle, corn, wine, fruits, and a slight cloth which the people make. One of these items must be traded for another as there is a great shortage of minted money.

We kept this ship and proceeded on our way. The next morning, 11 January, we sighted another sail. Giving chase, we took her later in the day. She was of much the same burden as the one taken the previous day. Her cargo, too, was similar, even to her having aboard a number of Negro slaves but in this instance all of the Negroes were women. She had other passengers, and five of these passengers were friars, one of whom was an Irishman. They were on their way upriver to Tucaman to take over a monastery which the bishop of Tucaman was causing to be built. Besides the friars, there were two Portuguese women, both of whom had been born in the River January.

From the crews of these prizes we had news of Master John Drake, whose bark, the *Francis,* had been a consort of Master Edward Fenton in 1583 [four years earlier] but had become separated from Master Fenton's fleet while close to the River Plate. We learned that Master Drake's ship had been cast away and lost, and that her company had been made captive by savages, all saving a few who had been slain by those same savages. The Englishmen had been badly used by their captors. However, Master Drake, Master Faireweather, and two or three others of their company had managed to escape in a canoe and reach the safety of a Spanish settlement.

On 12 January we came to Seal Island. On 14 January we were by Green Island where there is a safe road between it and the mainland, though one must take heed of a ledge of rock close to the isle. We lay there two days. Then 16 January we moved westward a league and took in eighteen tons of fresh water. Having watered, we set sail and returned to Seal Island so we could take seals for their meat. We arrived by the island on 22 January. But before we could carry out our purpose, a storm placed us in much danger. The violence of that storm was such we lost some of our anchors and cables. Too, and this amazed us greatly considering the latitude, it grew extremely cold. That we should find ourselves in such danger was due mostly to our own carelessness. We had spent sixteen days in the river's mouth, yet scarcely any soundings had been taken.

On 29 January we took into our ship a man who told us he was an Englishman by name of Miles Philips and that he had many years previous been left in the West Indies by Sir John Hawkins.

We departed the River Plate and held a course to the southward. On 1 February I took a sighting on the sun and found we were in the height of 38°. On 3 February I again took a sighting and discovered we were then in 41°. Four days later, our captain, our pilot, Master Anthony and myself, as well as others, left the *Clifford* and went aboard the admiral so that we might meet in council and decide on certain important matters having to do with the future of the voyage.

When we had gathered in Captain Withrington's cabin, filling it to overflowing, John Anthony, the master of the admiral, spoke to us at some length about things which he believed should be gone well into, things having to do with the safety of both our ships and our men. I give you his words as nearly as I can recall them:

"My masters, it is known to all of you that milord, the earl's intention was that this voyage, by the grace of God, should take us into the South Sea. It is also, as of this day, well known to all of you that various things are not now in favour of our proceeding with the action. The winds have been contrary and remain so. Each day the weather grows colder. Worse, our victuals are sadly diminished. We have, at very most, a two-month supply of biscuit. Our wine and beer are so near to being spent that we must, henceforth, depend entirely upon water. To be forced to drink naught but water in a region so cold as that where lies the Strait of Magellan would, I fear, greatly weaken our men, the more so should we be forced to winter there. That, in itself, could be a hazard sufficient to defeat the purpose of the voyage. These matters having already been well considered by our captain, Master Withrington, our pilot, Master Hood, and myself, we have all of us reached agreement. To our minds it is best for the good of the venture, the health of our men, and the safety of our ships that we return, without delay, to the coast of Brazil where, by God's grace, we shall be able to find victuals, wine, and other necessities.

"Besides, we have been given to understand by certain of our Portuguese captives, whom we have closely examined, that by our own endeavours, and God's help, we should, without great difficulty, be able to take the town of Baya [Salvador]. As proof they are telling us the truth about the lack of defences of the said town of Baya, they pledge the one thing of value left them—their lives. Now, should we go northward and, by taking Baya, revictual our ships, then we may spend three or even four months upon that coast. This we would, and could, do in peace and quiet, excepting of course that in the meantime we should happen upon some prize which would please milord, the earl. Come the spring, we could once more put forth and try to reach the South Sea. Should we do this, one and all of you may be assured we will, with God's assistance, not return to England empty-handed. Now if there be any one of you who has a better plan to offer, let him speak up, for, not only will we listen well to his words, but we will thank him for them."

To this good speech of Master John Anthony, Captain Lister replied:

"Masters Withrington and Anthony, both of you know, and know well, that in his last words to us milord, the earl, said that we should go to the South Sea. One thing only should be allowed to divert us from our purpose. It was this: Should we, on our way to the strait, meet with such rich prizes as would allow us to return to England with a profit of, at very least, £6,000. Until now, we have not come upon anything which would yield a tithe of that amount. Therefore, and as we are nearing the strait, I think we should go forward. For myself, I will consent to nothing else until such time as our lot is much worse than it now appears to be. My thinking is this: If one dies doing his duty this year, he cannot be held to account for what might happen next year. I speak for myself, and others too, when I say I choose death to returning empty of hand, and therefore in disgrace, to milord, the earl."

After Master Lister had spoken out so boldly, and bravely, both Captain Withrington and Master Anthony replied they were of the same mind as he. They too, they said, wished to see the voyage go forward, even though it might cost them their lives. But they still deemed it wiser we go back up the coast rather than to try wintering in either the strait or Port St. Julian. The meeting then ended but was resumed the following day which was 8 February. At this second meeting divers speeches were made, some in favour of our continuing our course, while about an equal number were for our returning northward. Then, and as arguing was getting us nowhere, a list of all of the victuals still in the ships was taken. The list revealed there was a greater store of victuals than at first was thought. Scarcely had we been told this than a wind began coming from out the north. It decided us. Hastily, we took out of the prizes those provisions which would best serve us. That done, we cast the prizes off and plied for the Strait of Magellan.

We held on our southerly course until 15 February when we found ourselves in the height of 44°. Then the favouring winds failed us. They were replaced by a wild storm from the south, which brought with it much rain and cold. This intemperate weather remained with us for six days, forcing us to take in all of our sails and lie ahull with the result we were driven back to the northward until we stood in 42°. On 20 February the storm eased somewhat. Immediately it showed signs of slacking, our admiral put his flag in the mizzen shrouds, his way of saying that he wished to speak with us. Not without difficulty, we hauled up close to the *Red Dragon*. When we were in hailing distance, Captain Withrington shouted across, telling us his entire company was for going northward to the coast of Brazil, as he and Master Anthony had first proposed.

At that, Captain Lister was displeased. He shouted back, saying that he and *his entire company* were still for trying to reach the strait. The admiral, though, cared not a whit what we thought. He stated the *Red Dragon* would be headed northward. The conversation ended there; the ships separated.

By the following day, 21 February, the weather was fair and the wind was such as would have allowed us to once more set sail for the strait. Our admiral, though, was leagues to the northward of us and holding course for Brazil. We were left with no choice other than to follow him. Later that day, though, we came up with him, and hailing him, Captain Lister again tried to persuade Captain Withrington to change his mind. Captain Withrington refused to be swayed, saying he had once more taken stock of his victuals and found their quantity and condition to be such he could do naught else than what he was doing. Having told us that, he had the *Red Dragon* crowd on all of her sails and haul away from us.

At that, those of us in the bark fell to considering whether we should follow the admiral or go, on our own, back toward the strait. Many things were weighed, including the condition of our men, our ship, and our ordnance. Honesty forced us into admitting that many of our men were weak and sick and, too, that both our ship and our ordnance were in a state of sad disrepair. Finally, but with reluctance, we decided to follow the admiral and to remain by him—at least until the spring.

The decision made, we remained with the fleet, proceeding northward without incident until 10 March. On that day our master's mate fell overboard. Despite our best efforts to save him, he was lost. Following that mishap, nothing untoward, or indeed anything to merit mention, happened until 28 March. On that date, and in the height of 21° south of the Equator, we espied a sail which we thought may have come through the Strait of Magellan and would, therefore, be richly laden. We gave chase, but unfortunately for us night was close at hand. We lost her in the darkness and never again caught sight of her. On 5 April a sighting showed us we stood in 16°. We had, at last, reached the land of Brazil.

That day, we brought up close to the admiral and our captain went aboard so he could confer with Captain Withrington. We stood in dire need of fresh water so the captains decided we should send small boats to the land. As result of their decision, eighteen men put off in the pinnace and a smaller ship's boat, taking butts which, when filled, would give us four tons of water. They were gone for three days, all of which time we lay offshore and worried. Finally though, they returned safely. When they were aboard, we set sail and later put into the road of Camana. Barely were we in than the most important Portuguese residing there came out to us in a canoe. From him, we learned that Camana was lacking in defences of any kind so we kept him with us while our men took cattle, hogs, water and wood at their pleasure and leisure. Then we departed and proceeded northward.

On 11 April we reached our goal, Baya. We were welcomed by the Portuguese firing two great pieces of ordnance at us which, fortunately, missed us and did no harm. These pieces were situated on a point at the entrance to the harbour. Once by them we proceeded, in safety, into the haven itself. But when we dropped our anchors the Portuguese once again began to shoot pieces at us, this time from the town itself. Fortune again favoured us. We were lying just beyond range of the pieces.

Eight ships, which number included a caravel and a large flyboat, lay in the harbour of Baya. None took kindly to us. All of them employed their ordnance against us but such was their marksmanship that we remained unharmed, receiving not so much as a single rent in our sails. In the meantime, not wishing to appear idle, we returned their shots, hitting some of the ships and dropping a few bullets into the town. Finally, we, and the Portuguese, ceased firing. The next morning, we would have closed with some of the ships, taken them, and by night hauled them out to sea; the wind, though, was so against us the idea was given over.

However, the next night there was a moon which made it nearly as bright as day. Manning four boats, we went in among the ships. The Portuguese shot at us, sending a hail of bullets about our ears. But when they perceived we cared not a whit for their bullets, they forsook their ships by crowding into their boats and heading for the land. A few, probably because there was not room for them in the boats, leaped overboard and swam to shore. We boarded most all of the ships, cutting the cables of three so they would drive. Four we decided to try taking past the ordnance on the point and so out to sea.

As we were about this, we had to pass close by the large flyboat, the one ship in the haven we had not boarded. This hulk straightaway let fly some bullets at us. Now for various reasons we had long been of the opinion this flyboat was not a Portuguese. We, therefore, hailed it, demanding to know to which country it belonged. They replied they were from Flushing, in Holland. Upon hearing that, we ordered them to follow us out to sea. More, we told them to bring with them two other ships which lay nearby. Thus with a fleet of seven captured vessels we passed safely out to sea, the great pieces on the point not firing at us at all, probably out of fear of hurting their own people. Unfortunately for us, though, these captured ships yielded us little of that we needed the most: victuals. As for merchandise, there was even less. All had recently been unloaded.

All of this was done on Easter eve. Purposely, we lay off the town all of the next day. Then by night, as we had fully expected, a boat from the town came out to us. This boat had in it a Dutchman and a Portuguese. They hailed us, and told us they had come to arrange ransom for the ships we had taken. Believing they might also have come to spy on us, to discover how weak or how strong we were, we would not allow them to return to shore but kept them aboard the *Clifford* the remainder of the night. In the morning, we took them across to the admiral. However, before anything regarding a ransom could be arranged, a great storm struck us. During its height we were so busily engaged in seeing to the safety of our own ships that two of the prizes broke their cables and slipped away. We sent boats to recover them, which proved a great mistake, for by doing so we lost, not only the prizes to the storm, but some of our seamen as well.

Also during the height of this storm two prisoners, Spaniards we had taken in the River Plate, squeezed through one of the cabin windows and swam ashore, something we had regarded as impossible considering the violence of the weather. By the morning of 19 April the storm had abated somewhat so we weighed our anchors and went to an island which lies to the northwest of the bay. There we stayed until the next day when, the weather having turned fine, a large company of us went ashore in order that we might help our carpenters set up a pinnace. We hoped we would be allowed to do this in peace. But on 23 April we were attacked by a considerable number of Indians who came at us from all directions at the same time. They let go a perfect hail of arrows, hurting some of our men. However, we made them retire quickly enough by giving them bullets in return for their arrows. We must have wounded and killed quite a few of them, for we could see several being either helped or carried away by their fellows.

On 26 April the carpenters finished the pinnace and we launched it. We were not sorry it was over with. The last day we worked on it we were forced to skirmish with a large force of men made up of both Portuguese and Indians. In this skirmishing, which lasted for quite some time, we fared better than did they. None of our men was lost or even wounded. One week later, fortune did not treat us so favourably. On 2 May, a boat from the *Red Dragon* with fourteen men aboard was sent ashore for water. As they were filling the butts, they were surprised by Indians to the number, or so it is said, of over 200. Two of our men were killed. The other twelve defended themselves so well they managed to escape and, surprisingly, even managed to bring off a number of water butts. In the opinion of many, the two men were lost through sheer negligence. The watering party should never have been sent ashore at that place and at that time.

On 5 May we were once more endangered by what one might well call a lack of circumspection on the part of our admiral. It was this way: Our ships had continued to lie offshore and from them we could see, at any time we chose to look, large numbers of bullocks grazing in the fields on the land. On 5 May Captain Withrington announced his intention of taking a company of sixty men ashore to hunt the bullocks for their fresh meat. In vain did Captain Lister try to acquaint him with the risks involved. But the admiral could not be dissuaded and so, in late afternoon, he put off from the fleet with a small bark, his own little caravel, the *Clifford's* pinnace, and a boat from the *Dutchman,* as we were wont to call the flyboat from Flushing.

When morning came, those of us aboard the *Clifford* could not see Captain Withrington or indeed any of his company because, during the night and as they had hunted, they had gone quite some distance inland. Meantime, the enemy had seen our boats lying near the shore and, surmising quite correctly their crews were ashore hunting bullocks, made plans which boded very ill indeed for Captain Withrington. They appeared from the direction of Baya in four caravals and a galley, each so filled with men there was standing-room for them only. Hugging the shore, the caravals bore down on our boats, their intentions, very plainly being, to capture the boats and by so doing leave our men stranded and at their mercy. Those of us on the *Clifford,* seeing what was about to take place, brought in our anchor and ran toward the shore. The *Dutchman,* at our command, did likewise. Alas, though, the water's depth kept us from getting close enough in to bring our pieces to bear on the enemy craft.

However, by then Captain Withrington and his men had appeared. Sensing the peril they were in, they hastily got aboard the boats. Then, in the very short time left them before the onslaught, they did a wise thing. All sixty of them went into the pinnace, which was not only the largest of their boats but had, as well, a small piece of ordnance. To make it more difficult for the enemy to board the pinnace, they lashed the Dutch boat to one side of it and the small caraval to the other. That done, they were as ready as they would ever be.

As the enemy vessels neared them they let go with their small piece, which shot was returned several-fold by enemy pieces, some of which had been loaded with hailshot. Too, and besides firing their pieces, the enemy beat loudly on drums and filled the air with wild yells. But when they attempted to board the pinnace our men gave them shots from their muskets, thrusts from their pikes, and blows from their swords. For a quarter hour the fight raged with amazing fury. So many of the enemy were slain it is difficult to believe that a company so small in number as ours could wreak such havoc upon one so much larger—unless we are willing to believe that the Giver of Victory, the Lord himself, blessed our small company by strengthening their arms, and their minds as well. As before stated, this battle raged for but a quarter hour. Then the enemy, admitting defeat, withdrew. It was the estimation of many that out of their original 200 and more, not above a score of them remained unscathed. In the bottoms of their vessels the dead lay tiered.

In this fierce conflict our dead were three only. True, others were wounded by shot or by arrow. But not one wound proved fatal. Thus did it please God, in His great goodness, to give victory to sixty Englishmen over a host several times their number. While still speaking of that fight, and more particularly about the losses of the enemy, our conjectures were borne out when, on the night following the battle, two Indians came out to us in a canoe. As they proved to be slaves who were running away from their masters, we welcomed them aboard, after which I fell to questioning them. They informed me that all of 400 men had gone forth in the vessels. But not more, they said, than thirty had returned to the town alive and uninjured. And now just one more item before passing on to other matters: Despite their having been so fiercely assaulted, our men had even managed to bring away with them the meat from seventeen young bullocks, which meat we greatly relished.

On 12 May I received a command from Captain Withrington, stating I should come aboard the *Red Dragon.* I complied. When I was on the *Dragon* the captain told me that the Dutchmen had demanded from him a bond, signed by his hand, which bond stated that upon our return to England they would be compensated, in full, and by the earl, for all merchandise taken out of their ship by us. Having already signed the bond, he wanted my opinion as to whether the earl would honour it. I advised him to get, if it were at all possible, the bond back, as I was far from certain milord would either honour it or be pleased with the captain for having given it. Having thus expressed my honest opinion, I went back to the *Clifford.*

On 13 May we sent out of our bark, and into the *Red Dragon,* various victuals that ship was short on. They consisted mainly of three butts of rice, one barrel of oatmeal and a barrel of oil. In return, we received little else than some sugar. On the day following that one, there was another meeting aboard the admiral. At the meeting it was decided we should make one final, all-out attempt at taking the town of Baya. We also planned on how to go about it.

Soon after, and in accordance with our plans, we placed most all of the men of our combined companies into the small boats and pinnaces and set forth for the town. But before we got close in, such a strong wind set against us that we could make no headway. We had, therefore, to give up the venture and return to the ships. This was perhaps well for us, when one takes into consideration the thousands of Indians and Portuguese we would have had to face—to say nothing of their artillery.

For a whole week following our failure to so much as reach the town let alone assault it, we employed the greater part of our time raiding the various plantations which lie along the coast on either side of Baya. From them, and the villages too, the people always fled at sight of us, therefore we could have what we wished, which was little else than sugar. When we had taken the sugar, we would set fire to the buildings. During that week of raiding, there appeared a caraval which we chased and took. She was empty. But she had three pieces of ordnance, iron falconets, which we took. Then we set her afire. On that same day some of our men who were in one of the small prizes ran too close in to the shore and, as result, went aground at low tide. There they lay for the space of four hours or more. Meantime, the Portuguese, who were keeping close watch on us, perceived what had happened and sent five caravals, each filled with men, along the shore toward the stranded prize. However, we frightened them off by going so close in with the *Clifford* we could have used our ordnance on them. We remained there, on guard, until at half flood the prize floated free and that was the end of the matter.

On 19 May we once more set sail for the purpose of going into the road of Baya. Our intention on this occasion was not to harm anyone, but rather to send our pinnace to the town under a flag of truce to see if an exchange of prisoners could be arranged. The Portuguese had four of our men who had been driven ashore during the storm when they had been sent to recover a prize. We had a few of their men, taken with the prizes. But no sooner had we neared the town than we were shot at. In return, we let go twenty-seven pieces at them and then, in defiance of their artillery, we anchored in the road. There we lay for the night. Come the morning, the admiral sent a Negro with letters from the prisoners, which letters informed the governor of Baya of the proposed exchange. We thought the governor would readily agree, as we had more of their men than they had of ours.

We were due for a surprise. Such was the hardheartedness of the Portuguese governor, that he sent to us two Indians, bearing letters telling us he would not even entertain the idea of an exchange of prisoners. Included were a few words for his countrymen. He advised them to bear the ill fortune of their captivity with patience. The letters did contain one offer: The Portuguese would buy back one of the prizes. Our admiral answered him, saying that unless we got our men back we would not deal with them in any way. That evening, we weighed anchors, putting out to sea for as much as half a league. The following morning we put out sail and went to an island which lies some twelve leagues to the south of Baya. Our purpose in going there was so we could take in wood and water. While we were about those tasks, we sighted a canoe containing a Portuguese and six Indians. Our pinnace gave chase to this canoe but, in taking it, they were forced to kill one of the Indians. They brought the other six back.

We examined the Portuguese and he confessed he knew of a ship, one laden with meal and other commodities, which was hiding from us in a nearby creek. Two days later, with our captive guiding us, we found the ship. She proved a most worthy prize, as she was new and of the burden of 120 tons. Too, and as we had been told, she was laden chiefly with meal, though she also had in her fourteen chests of sugar. We brought her out of the creek and to the fleet where her cargo was divided among our ships, according to the needs of each.

On 30 May, a party of sixteen or seventeen from the *Dutchman* went ashore in their boat for water. They were ambushed by as many as fifty or sixty Portuguese and an equal, or even greater, number of Indians, all of them armed with either arquebuses or bows. The master and the purser of the Dutch ship were slain. The remaining Dutchmen escaped in their boat but there was not a single one of them who did not suffer wounds. Their misfortune was a warning to all of us that we must be most careful when landing, for whatever purpose, anywhere in the vicinity of Baya.

On the next day, 31 May, we emptied one of the prizes and cast her off, letting her drive wherever the winds willed. Later the same day, our captain, Master Lister, headed a watering party of forty well-armed men and took them ashore to the very spot where the men from the Dutch ship had been ambushed. As we expected, a considerable number of Portuguese were guarding the watering place. But upon seeing the strength of our company, to say naught of our resolution, the cowardly villains refused to fight. Instead, they ran for the hills. At that, Master Lister took nine men and pursued them well into the land. He finally came back to us, after which we watered without interference.

On 3 June, Master Lister, who still had a great desire to carry out the original purpose of the voyage, that is, to pass through the Strait of Magellan, asked for and received an audience with Captain Withrington. During their discussion, Master Lister requested that he be given six butts of wine, one barrel of oil, and four barrels of meat. Too, he wished to make an exchange of men. He would give the admiral various of our landsmen for Master Hood, the pilot for the strait, and eight seamen of the better sort. If the admiral would allow him those things, said Master Lister, he would, with God's help, take the *Clifford* through the strait and on to the South Sea.

Master Lister returned to us in an unhappy frame of mind. The admiral had, and very mightily, denied him each and all of his requests.

On 7 June we rid ourselves of our prizes. One we burned; the other we simply cast off. The following day we put to sea, but were promptly driven back by foul weather. On 10 June we were signalled and told to come aboard the *Red Dragon*. Once there and in the great cabin, the admiral wasted no time in telling us what was in his mind. He said that for want of victuals and able seamen, milord's intended voyage to the South Sea must be given over. Instead, he said, we would go home by way of the West Indies and the Azores in the hope a prize, or prizes, rich enough to defray the expenses of the voyage, and so satisfy milord, would fall our way. Master Lister, myself, and others as well, listened to

Captain Withrington's words in grief and silence. He was our admiral. We had no choice but to obey him. Within the hour, the fleet was under sail and following the coast northward.

On 16 June we sighted a sail which our pinnace pursued and drove ashore upon an island. Her crew having fled to the land, the men from the pinnace boarded her without difficulty, but they found little of worth to us in her, excepting nine chests of sugar, a hog, and thirty-five pieces of pewter. Our men took those things, then departed, leaving the ship high on the sands. After that we kept farther out from the land, not raising the coast again until 1 July, upon which date I took a sighting on the sun and found we were in 10° 22′ south. On 7 July we were off Fernambuck [Recife] in latitude 7° 50′; we would have gone in to it on the chance of taking prizes but the weather prevented our doing so. In fact, a strong wind from the south caused us to overshoot the place. Our pinnace, though, managed to get so close her master later declared he could see the topmasts of the ships lying in the road.

On 20 July I took the sun in 5° 50′, confirming that we were by then upwards of fifty leagues to the northward of Fernambuck. At that time the ships were having great difficulty keeping within sight of each other. In particular, the admiral, a fast sailer, was outdistancing the rest of us. True, there were occasions when we would manage to bring the *Clifford* up close to him—but never so near that we could exchange signals. Always, or so it seemed to us, the *Red Dragon* would choose that time to crowd on extra sail and pull away. Finally, we concluded that Master Withrington did not wish our company, so we decided that, henceforth, we would look after ourselves. That decision reached, Captain Lister, on 24 July, conferred with the entire company as to what course we should set. The greater number of the men were of the opinion that, considering our lack of victuals and fresh water, we should try to get home by the shortest route possible.

On 27 July we took stock of our water. As we had but nine casks and we were fifty in number, Captain Lister put us on a daily allowance of a pint of water per man. On 1 August we found ourselves in 5° north latitude; all of August we continued on a homeward course but, nearing the end of the month, a sorrowful accident befell us. The *Dutchman* had fallen quite some distance behind, though we could still sight her hull down. Then there came a complete calm. As we lay there motionless, we witnessed the hulk take fire and burn with, we fully suspect, the loss of her entire crew. We were, on account of the distance and the calm, helpless to aid them.

On 29 September we reached the coast of England, ending the voyage.

Sarracoll left a few important facts out of his narrative. For instance, he tells us they left Plymouth with four ships: *Red Dragon, Clifford, Roe,* and the fine pinnace, the *Dorothy*. But he never tells us what became of either the *Roe* or the *Dorothy*.

Sarracoll is harsh in his judgement of Captain Withrington. Probably he was correct in his inference that Withrington was over-cautious. There seems no good reason why he should have got no farther southward than latitude 44°. At that point in the voyage, his expedition should have been in as good, or better condition, than was Drake's.

Lister was quite different, certainly a more impulsive man than Withrington. His had been a life of high adventure. He had even spent several years as a captive of the Moors. When Sarracoll says that Lister was for continuing the voyage even though it might cost him his life, it may be accepted. He has been described as a "rashly valiant captain."

Lister maintained his connections with the Earl of Cumberland. In 1589 the earl sailed from Plymouth in command of a privateering fleet. Lister was one of his captains. When they reached the Azores they were joined by Captain John Davis, the same Davis whose voyages to the Northwest appear in this book. At Santa Maria the English found two ships which were lying under the shelter of shore guns; indeed, the people had brought the ships in so close to shore in the hope of saving them from Cumberland's ships that one was actually aground.

Despite the apparent dangers, Lister and Davis went boldly in and boarded the prizes. Davis, though, more prudent than Lister, abandoned his prize when he saw that taking it off would be very costly. He had picked the ship which was aground. Lister, under heavy fire from the shore, began to bring his prize out. Unfortunately, it hung up on a bar while still within range of the enemy cannon. In the ensuing fight, which both the earl and Davis joined, eighty Englishmen were lost. But Lister brought the prize ship off. In that battle the earl gained considerable experience and a minor wound.

Lister's luck, though, was running out. On his way back to England, aboard what has been described as a rich prize, he reached Mount's Bay on the coast of Cornwall. There a great storm caused the ship to founder. Lister and all but six men were lost.

The Earl of Cumberland refused to be discouraged. In 1591 he set out on another voyage. On this voyage various prizes were taken, but again ill fortune dogged him. Two of the prizes were lost, one foundering in a storm and the other retaken by the Spanish when it was forced into Corunna by lack of food and water. In the end, this voyage too brought little reward to the earl.

Although the big prize always eluded him or was snatched from him by fate, the earl persisted, making in all, or causing to be made, close to a dozen privateering voyages. These included attacks on Spanish towns in the West Indies. On one occasion he captured the town of San Juan, Puerto Rico. On that foray, his fleet consisted of eighteen sail, the largest ever assembled by a private individual.

So much did the Earl of Cumberland's swashbuckling exploits appeal to the English people that, whenever he appeared on the streets of London, he was given the acclaim usually accorded royalty. In 1606, at age forty-eight, he died and was buried at Skipton in Yorkshire.

PART THREE

Voyages Around the Globe

ARCTIC OCEAN
PRIME MERIDIAN
ARCTIC CIRCLE
HUDSON BAY
NORTH AMERICA
BRISTOL
PLYMOUTH
EUROPE
CALIFORNIA
ATLANTIC OCEAN
C. St. Lucas
Mazatlán
Chaccalla
Santiago Bay
Acatlan
Acapulco
Guatulco
CARIBBEAN SEA
Rio de Oro
TROPIC OF CANCER
Cape Blanco
AFRICA
St. Vincent
Cape Verde Is.
Trinidad
Guyana (Guiana)
SOUTH SEA
EQUATOR
Gulf of Guayaquil
Paita
SOUTH AMERICA
Callao
BRAZIL
Baya (Salvador)
Arica
St. Helena
Cabo Frio
TROPIC OF CAPRICORN
Morro Moreno
San Sebastian Is.
Santos
PACIFIC OCEAN
Quintero
Valparaiso
Isle of Santa Maria
Is. of Mocha
Cape of Good Hope
Port Desire
Cape Deseado
Cape Froward
STRAIT OF MAGELLAN

The first voyage of

Thomas Cavendish

as told by Master Francis Pretty

Thomas Candish or, as it is usually spelled, Cavendish, was born at Trimley St. Mary in Suffolk in 1560. For a time he attended Corpus Christi College, Cambridge, but left when, at the age of about nineteen, he came into a large inheritance. At once he took himself to Court and before long his inheritance was sadly depleted. It was then the young Cavendish decided to replenish his fortune by taking to the sea. At his own expense he fitted out a ship called the *Tiger* and in it, under Sir Richard Grenville, he took part in Sir Walter Raleigh's attempt to colonize Virginia in 1584-85. Cavendish, however, did not winter in Virginia. Instead, he tried his hand at buccaneering in the West Indies and returned to England the following year. He did not profit greatly from this venture. What he did gain was experience, which he shortly decided to put to use. Thrilled, as were so many in England, by the successful round-the-world voyage of that "deare pyrat," Francis Drake, Cavendish decided to emulate him.

He had built and outfitted for two years two ships, the *Desire* and the *Content*. With them and a bark, the *Hugh Gallant*, he started out. The story of Cavendish's prosperous voyage around the world—his was the third ship ever to accomplish the feat—is ably told by Master Francis Pretty of Eye in County Suffolk, a gentleman who sailed on the voyage. Pretty is careful never to say anything derogatory about Cavendish. The next man to write about him is not so kind and understanding. John Janes, who wrote of Cavendish's last voyage, is critical and, in one instance, quite bitter. But Pretty too, probably without realizing it, supplies us with a great many clues as to the nature of Thomas Cavendish, who even by sixteenth-century standards was a cold and ruthless man.

We departed out of Plymouth on Thursday, 21 July, 1586, with three sail, to wit: the *Desire* of 120 tons; the *Content* of sixty tons; and the *Hugh Gallant*, a bark of forty tons burden. In this small fleet there were 123 persons, together with furniture and victuals judged sufficient to support them for two years. Our general was the Worshipful Master Thomas Cavendish of Trimley in the County of Suffolk.

On Tuesday, 26 July, we were forty-five leagues off Cape Finisterre in Spain, at which time we met five Biscayan, fishermen returning, or so we thought, from the Grand Banks of Newfoundland. We fought with them for some three hours but, the night coming on, the darkness saved them and we saw them no more. Four days later, 1 August, we raised Fuertaventura, one of the Canary Islands. On 7 August, a Sunday, we were by the Rio de Oro on the Barbary coast. The following day we fell in with Cape Blanc. Off this cape there were numerous fishing vessels called cantars, and we would have gone among them but a strong northerly wind thwarted us. On 15 August we were in the height of the Cape Verde Islands but, by our estimation, some fifty leagues to the eastward of them. The 25 August we fell in with the point, or cape, which lies on the south side of the Bay of Sierra Leone, a place our Master Brewer knew very well as he had been there before. That being so, the next day he took the *Content* close in to the land and to where she, and the entire fleet, could lie in a safe road about a league from the point. We were then about 930 leagues distant from England.

The day following our arrival and as we lay in the road, two Negroes came out to us in their canoe. By hand signs, they let us know there was a Portuguese ship lying further up the harbour. The *Hugh Gallant*, the smallest of our ships and the one least likely to run aground, was sent to look for the Portuguese ship. The *Hugh Gallant* sailed perhaps as many as four leagues up the bay, but her company was afraid to proceed farther without a pilot so they returned to us without having seen the ship they sought. It was well they gave over the search when they did. Later we learned, from a Portuguese we made captive, that the waters beyond where the *Hugh Gallant* had gone are very dangerous.

On the Sunday the general sent the ship's musicians, and others of the company as well, ashore, so the musicians could play and dance for the Negroes and thereby gain their confidence. They remained with the Negroes all of the afternoon, partly in the hope they would receive further news regarding the Portuguese ship. They heard nothing more about her but, as they were returning to the shore, they had the good fortune to espy a white man, a Portuguese, lying hidden, as he thought, among some bushes. They seized him and brought him aboard.

Before examining our prisoner, we first bound him fast in order to make certain that what he told us was the truth. He said his name was Emmanuel and that he was by trade a caulker whose ship had been cast away and lost so that he and two others had been living for quite some time among the Negroes. He admitted knowing of the ship we were seeking. But he warned us that where she lay it would be most dangerous for us to try going. We believed him and decided to bother ourselves no more about the ship.

Monday, 29 August, our general took seventy men and went to the town of the Negroes, finding it to be a marvelously well-built place of about 100 houses, standing in an open space in the forest. The walls of these houses were of mud and the yard of each had a paling [fence]. Both the houses and the streets were very clean. When the Negroes saw the general and his men approaching, they became alarmed and fled into the woods. From there they shot arrows at us, hurting three or four of our men. Though we worried that the arrows might be poisoned, none of the wounded died. We revenged ourselves by burning three of their houses. We also took a few things which suited our fancy.

On 1 September almost our entire company went ashore and to a watering place so the men could wash their clothing, which they did, remaining there for several hours in peace and quiet. The next day they went to the same place. This time, though, Negroes had concealed themselves in the surrounding bushes. However, one of the carpenters having gone into the edge of the trees so he could do some special business in private, spied the Negroes and gave the alarm. At that the Negroes all rushed out of the forest, shooting arrows and otherwise attacking our men. As they were hastening into the boats and putting off, several seamen were wounded, as was a soldier named Pickman who was struck in the thigh by an arrow. Pickman, in trying to pluck the arrow out, broke it so that the head remained buried in his flesh. Later and in order to avoid the misery of having the arrowhead cut out of his thigh, he lied to the surgeon by saying he had removed all of it. The arrowhead was poisoned. That night Pickman's leg, belly, and private parts all became marvellously swollen and turned black as ink. In the morning he was dead.

On 3 September most of our company spent the day fishing from their boats and the catch was good. They also went into the trees ashore and plucked fruit, including lemons. On 6 September we left the road where we had been lying for upwards of a fortnight and went to one of the islands of the Cape Verdes where we anchored about two miles from shore and remained overnight. The next day we sent a boat clear round the island, taking soundings and seeking a place where we might water. We found a town on the east end of the island, which the Negroes sometimes use but was then deserted. On the north side of the island we found various places where water might be had. The entire island is wooded, except for small clearings where the people have their houses. Each house usually has a few plantain trees growing about it. The plantain is, we discovered, a most delicious fruit. The Cape Verdes, from our experience and observation, appears to be a region where thunder storms occur daily, bringing with them a great deal of rain. This is probably because they lie so close to the Equator.

We departed from there on 10 September at about three of the clock in the afternoon. On the last day of October we raised Cabo Frio lying on the north side of the entrance to the River January in Brazil and, by running twenty-four leagues to the west-southwest from Cabo Frio, we fell in with a great mountain. This mountain has a most distinctive top. A high, round knob at its summit gives one the impression a town has been built there. The next day, 1 November, we went in between the Island of San Sebastion and the mainland and came to anchor in a road close to the island.

After being at sea for so long, there were many things which needed doing, so a forge was set up ashore and for the next three weeks we were kept busy at a variety of tasks: the coopers made hoops and repaired the water casks; we fitted together, and launched, a pinnace we had brought in pieces with us from England. As well, we took on goodly supplies of both wood and water.

While we were about these necessary chores, and others too, there happened along a canoe which had come from the River January. Bound for St. Vincent, it was owned by a Portuguese and was being rowed by six naked Indians. By chance, the Portuguese knew the master of the *Desire*, Christopher Hare, the two having met when Master Hare had visited St. Vincent in the *Minion*, a ship of London, in 1581. Master Hare inquired about an Englishman, a John Whithal, who dwells at St. Vincent. When told that Whithal was still there, and well, an invitation was sent to him to come visit us. As St. Vincent was but twenty leagues to southward of where we lay, we had hopes that if Whithal came to us arrangements might be made whereby it would be possible for us to purchase fresh victuals. By letter, we acquainted Whithal of our intentions, taking care to assure him that we would pay for anything we received. But something must have prevented his coming to us. We waited ten days and then, as there was still no sign of him and, too, as we were finished with the work on the ships, we left. The date of our departure was 23 November.

On 16 December we were in the height of 47° 20′ [south latitude], and close in to a high, steep shoreline. We continued to run southward along this shore until the next afternoon when we entered a harbour which our general named Port Desire. This harbour was ideal for us in many ways, chief among them being the fact it is a good place to ground ships on account of its beaches and the vast difference between the high and the low of its tides. It was at once decided we would grave [scrape] and trim our ships there. Its other advantages included two islands, one of which had a large number of seals upon it, while the other had an even greater number of big fowls of the sort that cannot fly and have burrows in the ground not unlike those made by rabbits. Both fowls and seals are good to eat, though the latter are so large they are difficult to slay. One important item for our comfort, though, was lacking in this otherwise excellent haven: drinking water.

To overcome this difficulty, we went to a green valley on the mainland and at a distance of about 800 paces from where our ships lay. There we dug a shallow well, a pit really, but it supplied us with an abundance of sweet water. It also brought us in contact with the people of the country, something which proved not to our advantage as will be seen.

The truth is, until 24 December, Christmas Eve, we did not know there were people in the vicinity. We had neither seen any of them or indeed any sign the land was inhabited. That being so, two of our company, a man named John Garge and boy called Lurch, felt themselves safe in going to the watering place to wash their clothing. But Indians had concealed themselves nearby and, rising up, they shot their arrows at Garge and the boy. Both were wounded. Garge was hit in the knee, Lurch in the shoulder. Though their hurts were painful, they saved themselves by fleeing back toward the shore. The Indians, who are as wild as deer, did not follow.

Upon learning of what had happened, the general took between sixteen and twenty men and, going ashore, he pursued the Indians far inland, this despite the fact his company was vastly outnumbered by the people of the country. These Indians would appear to be of very great stature. We measured a footprint of one of them; it was eighteen inches in length. During our stay at Port Desire, we learned other things about them as well. For instance, when a man dies he is brought to the cliffs overlooking the sea, and there they bury him in a grave made from stones. Beside him in his grave are placed his weapons, his bow and arrows and his darts. Before being put there they are painted red. Then last, the gravestones are also painted red. Apparently these people are much attracted to that colour. The few we saw had daubs and streaks of it on both their faces and their bodies.

We set sail from Port Desire itself on 28 December. However, we only took the ships three leagues to the southward and to where there is an island which has many of the large, wingless fowls. We slew a considerable number of the birds, then salted their flesh so it would keep. That done, on the following day we continued the voyage. On 30 December we sighted a rock lying about five leagues from the mainland. Its shape reminded many of us of the Eddystone near Plymouth. A sighting told us the rock stands in

48° 30′ south. On 3 January we fell in with a great white cape in the height of 52° 45′. About one league to the southward of this cape there is a long, low beach which reaches to the entrance of the dangerous Strait of Magellan. As the weather chose that time to become foul, we anchored under the cape. However, its shelter was not sufficient to save us entirely from damage. During the three days we lay there we lost an anchor and suffered various other inconveniences.

On 6 January 1587 we put into the strait. The next day we took a Spaniard who told us his name was Hernando, and that he and twenty-three others were all still remaining alive of 400 men who had been left there three years before. Famine and disease, he said, had taken the rest. Later that same day we passed through what is the narrowest part of the strait, which lies about fourteen leagues westward of the entrance. There, our Spaniard showed us the wreck of an English ship. We decided it must be a bark called the *John Thomas*. After examining, and leaving the wreck, we passed another ten leagues into the strait and came to what is called the Isle of Penguins. We stopped, slew some of the birds and salted them, then we passed on. The next day, 9 January, we arrived by the deserted City of King Philip, whose site had been carefully chosen so that it might guard the strait. Though well planned, it had only been partially built. Indeed its four greatest pieces had never been mounted on their carriages; instead they had been buried in the ground. We dug them up and had them for ourselves.

There was wood and water at King Philip's City, but little else for the use of man excepting mussels and limpets in the sea and a few fowls and deer on the land. According to our captive, the 400 and odd persons who had been left to garrison the place had, at first, put forth great effort. They had built a church, made strict laws and erected a gibbet for those who would not keep them. But misfortune had ever been their companion so that it would appear it was not God's will the strait should be fortified against all other nations but Spain. First, the Indians resented their coming and attacked the Spaniards whenever they ventured far from their fortress. Their victuals became exhausted and could not be replenished. That being so, they died like dogs until, in the end and when we arrived, there was the stench of death throughout the city, for bodies lay unburied both in the houses and on the streets. When finally their city had become untenantable, the last remnant of the people had taken their arquebuses and left, intending to try to make their way back through the strait and then northward up the coast to the River Plate. We took Hernando with us. The fate of the other twenty-three we do not know. Our general, with good reason, renamed the place Port Famine.

From Port Famine our course was, of necessity, southwesterly until we arrived by Cape Froward which stands in 54° and is the most southerly part of the strait. Beyond Cape Froward the strait trends, sharply, to the west and the north. Having rounded this cape and gone five leagues beyond it, we came to a cove which, because it had such an abundance of mussels, we named Mussel Cove. As the wind at that time was out of the west and very strong, we anchored and stayed there for six days. On 21 January we left and proceeded for another ten leagues, coming then to a sandy bay on the north side. Our general named it Elizabeth Bay and there we buried one of our men, a carpenter whose name was Grey. Leaving Elizabeth Bay on the afternoon of 22 January, we had gone about two leagues only when we came to a freshwater river. We anchored by its mouth as our general had a mind to explore it somewhat. Very shortly thereafter he, and several others of us, put off in a boat and went up the river for perhaps as much as a league, finding that it ran through a pleasant country which had soil covering its rocks. This was unusual as, from our observations, the strait is, for the greater part, bounded by craggy hills, bare rocks, and monstrous mountains.

On our journey upriver we met savages who were not afraid of us and who came to the water's edge in order that they might converse with us. They put on a great pretence of friendliness, making all manner of signs in their efforts to persuade us that we should go farther upstream. But we were not deceived. In our opinion they were cannibals and not to be trusted in any way. In their very hands we saw proof of this: They had Spanish knives and the points of some of their darts had been fashioned from the steel of Spanish swords. From those things we knew they had preyed on the people at Port Famine. Once the general became convinced of this, he lost all compassion for them and ordered us to shoot our pieces at them. We did, killing several. We then turned our boat about and returned to the ships. The river—it bears the name of St. Jerome—lies about thirty-four leagues from the western end of the strait. The entire length of the strait, in our judgement, is about ninety leagues.

We left the mouth of the River St. Jerome and passed a few leagues farther along the strait. Then the westerly winds became so violent we could make no headway at all against them and we were forced into a harbour. We lay there for an entire month, every day of which the weather treated us most vilely. It rained and rained. And betimes the winds were so wild we feared for both our anchors and our cables. Had we lost them, we might very well have lost our ships, to say naught of our lives also. During the days we lay there, we conserved our victuals by subsisting for the most part on mussels and limpets. It was 23 February before the weather permitted us to leave. Once underway, though, our progress was good. The following day, 24 February, we cleared the strait and entered the South Sea. A sighting taken on the sun at noon of that happy day revealed we were in the height of 52° 40′. We immediately set course to the north.

On 1 March, by which time we had reached the height of 49° 30′, such a storm descended upon us that during the night and the darkness the *Hugh Gallant* became separated from the other ships. For the space of three or four days this storm raged and, as our bark was leaky, we stood constantly by the pumps. We never slept. We scarce found the opportunity to eat. When the weather, thanks be to God, quieted to where we could once more put back onto the prescribed course, we proceeded northward, hoping we would at some time or other become reunited with the *Desire* and the *Content*. The event we so longed for, by grace of God, did finally take place—but not before ten anxious days had gone by and we had passed northward until we were by the Island of St. Mary. That island stands in about 37°.

It was, to be exact, the morn of 15 March when we sighted the other ships. When we brought up with them, we were told that they had lain for two days off the Island of Mocha, about twenty-five leagues to the southward of St. Mary. At Mocha a boat from the *Content* had gone ashore but, upon its men landing, they were at once assailed by Indians who shot arrows at them. Our men gave answer with their calivers, and the Indians fled. They have, it seems, a great fear of arquebuses and such. We later learned that our men had been mistaken for Spaniards, for whom the Indians have a great enmity as the Spaniards have made various attempts to conquer them, mainly because their land is reputed to be rich in gold.

On the afternoon of the day when we became reunited, we brought all three ships into a good road on the west side of the Island of St. Mary and anchored them there for the night. The next morning the general, with eighty armed men, went ashore. He expected resistance. Instead, the Indians who dwell there mistook us for Spaniards and, as the Spaniards have long since subdued them, they greeted us. Two of their chiefs made speeches of welcome, after which we were guided to where the Spaniards had erected a church, complete with altars and crosses. Of more interest to us than the church were three storehouses which stood nearby. All three were filled with bushel caddies, which caddies had been cleverly woven from straw. Each contained wheat or barley or corn. This grain was as fair and as clean, and indeed as good in every way, as any I have ever seen in England. Besides the grain, there were a number of caddies filled with potatoes. All of these items had been stored against the day when the Spaniards would come to collect tribute. As well as growing grain, these people also raise considerable numbers of hogs and hens. But such is the state of complete slavery the Spaniards have imposed upon them that they will not dare to eat so much as a hen without first getting permission from their masters. One thing the Spaniards have done for these people: They have made Christians of them.

Our general, having fully assessed the situation, had the two chiefs come aboard the *Desire* where he treated them royally and made them merry with wine. In the meantime, we went about revictualling our ships, a task which took over two days, but even then we did not empty the storehouses, for we left behind us as much as we took. When finished, we put the chiefs ashore and departed, running to the north-northeast for about ten leagues. Then with the night coming on, we took in our sails and lay-to until the morning.

We continued this practice of sailing by day and stopping by night, until 30 March, at which time we arrived in the bay of Quintero which stands in 33° 50′. We came to anchor close to the shore and not far from where a considerable herd of cattle, and one lone horse, were grazing on a hillside. At first, we thought the cattle were unattended but they were not. Their herder must have been asleep, for, of a sudden, we saw a man leap to his feet, run to the horse, jump onto its back and gallop madly off.

Our general, taking with him thirty men, all of them armed with arquebuses, landed. Included in the company was Hernando, the starving Spaniard we had rescued in the strait. This man, having taken an oath that he would never desert us, was fully trusted by the general who thought he might be of use as an interpreter. Very shortly there was need for an interpreter, for scarcely had the general and his men landed than three horsemen were seen approaching. However, they drew their mounts to a sliding stop while some hundreds of paces from us. Seeing they would come no nearer, the general sent two of our men, each armed with an arquebus, and Hernando forward to parley with the riders. Hernando, from some little distance, spoke to them for a great long time then he, and his two companions, came back to us. Hernando told the general the horsemen said they would be willing to let us have all the victuals we wished. Upon hearing that, the general sent Hernando and three of our own men back to the horsemen to complete arrangements. But this time the men on the horses were very wary. They shouted to Hernando, saying they would allow only one man to come near them at a time. When Hernando had given this message to our men, they conferred at length but finally agreed that he should go forward alone. He did. But no sooner was he to the horsemen than he leaped up behind one of them. Then the lot of them spun their horses about and galloped off. Thus did the vile Hernando, despite all of his oaths never to forsake us and to die by our sides if necessary, play us false.

Our general, seeing how he had been dealt with, took no action that day, except to keep a good watch while we took on some water. But the following morning he had Captain Havers and sixty men march into the country with orders to seek out the town of the Spaniards and loot and burn it. We tried to carry out his orders. We marched clear to the foot of the mountains which, on that part of the coast, rise up about eight miles from the sea. But we saw no sign of a town. What we did see, though, were great numbers of horses and cattle, as well as hares, rabbits, and wildfowl. Having reached the foot of the mountains we were weary so we rested by a river, drank of its sweet water, and then began our return march, taking a different route in the hope we might still catch sight of their town. Again we did not see it. But we saw Spaniards. Far distant from us we espied a large body of horsemen but they made no move to attack us.

The next day, 1 April 1587, twenty-seven of us went ashore and to a pit about a quarter mile from the shore to fill some butts with water. As we expected no trouble from the Spaniards, only fifteen of us were armed. But scarcely had we begun to fill the butts than fully 200 horsemen came galloping toward us out of the hills. So quickly did they come upon us that they rode through us, cutting off twelve of our men from the main body. All of the twelve were either killed or made captive. The rest of us made it in safety to rocks along the shore, where the horsemen could not get at us. From the rocks we skirmished with them for more than an hour, killing at least a score. Then soldiers from the ships came to our rescue and, at the mere sight of them, the Spaniards retired.

Despite our losing the twelve men, we continued to lie in the road. Nor did we allow the constant threat of attack to keep us from completing the task of replenishing our fresh water. Instead, we just kept better watch while we were about it. On 5 April we left Quintero and, stopping only to take on some penguins from an island about five leagues away, we held on course to the northward, making such headway that by 15 April we were athwart a place called Morro Moreno which lies in 23° 30′ and has a very good harbour. Here the general took thirty of us ashore where, upon our landing, we were met by a considerable number of Indians, each bearing upon his back either a skin of [filled with] water or a bundle of wood. Once again we had been so fortunate as to be mistaken for Spaniards who are held in marvellous awe by these simple people.

We did nothing to enlighten them as to their error, with the result they were pleased to guide us to their village which lay some two miles from the harbour. There, we saw their women, their houses, and other things having to do with their way of life. They are a most primitive people whose dwellings are but huts of brush, having for floors the skins of animals laid upon the ground. The bow is their main weapon, and when a man dies, it, and arrows for it, are laid beside him in his grave. Their food, from our observation, appears to be little else than poorly cured, and therefore stinking, fish. However, and in contrast to the crudity of their other belongings, their canoes are skilfully made and their mastery of them is such they will venture miles out to sea in them. As there was precious little these people had which interested us, and even less to tempt us, we soon went back to our ships and resumed our voyage northward.

For the week following our departure from Morro Moreno, little out of the ordinary occurred. But on 23 April matters livened. Early on the morning of that day we found ourselves nearing the sizable town of Arica. The *Desire* and the *Hugh Gallant* were together and leading; the *Content* was well back. The *Content*'s company, while they were still about fourteen leagues to the southward of Arica, sighted a Spanish ship which was close in to the shore. They went in, took the ship, and discovered she was laden with jars of wine. They spent some time removing a portion of this wine and putting it into the *Content*, then they released the Spanish ship and hastened after us.

Meantime, those of us in the other ships had approached Arica and, when almost at the entrance to the road we, too, sighted a Spanish ship, a small bark. Immediately the Spaniards saw us bearing down on them, they deserted the bark and rowed toward the land in their small boat. We, too, resorted to our boats. A boat from the *Hugh Gallant* boarded the bark while the admiral's pinnace took off in pursuit of the Spaniards, hoping to overtake them before they reached land. They failed their purpose. The Spaniards reached the land, beached their craft, and ran in the direction of the town. At that, the pinnace boldly entered the harbour where a ship of at least 100 tons was lying at anchor. But the town had already been warned and was in arms against us. As the pinnace was making its way to the ship, four shots were fired at it, all of them missing. The men in the pinnace did not allow the shots to deter them. They boarded the ship but found neither men nor goods in it.

Shortly thereafter, the *Desire* and the *Hugh Gallant* were brought into the road. Had the *Content* been with us, the general would have landed and tried taking the town. In her absence he felt we lacked both the men and the small boats to assure the success of such a bold undertaking. We, therefore, lay in the road until the *Content* came up. By then, it was too late to attempt an assault. As said before, Arica is a populous place. Besides, it is probable they drew men from other towns, for such an array of men presented themselves to our gaze that our general very quickly cast aside any thought of a landing of any sort. But as we lay in the road, the Spaniards kept shooting their ordnance at us and we returned them shot for shot, with no damage done, at least not to us. The Spanish gunners were far from skilled. This was demonstrated beyond all doubt when our pinnace went close in to board and take a small bark which lay hard against the shore. Shots rained about the pinnace. But there was not a single hit and the prize was brought safely away.

After the above happening, our general sent a boat, one bearing a flag of truce, to the shore. His purpose in doing so was to offer the Spaniards a deal. They could have their ships back if we could have our men who had been taken captive at Quintero. Their answer was a forceful *no*! They explained their position by stating they had been expressly forbidden, by the king's viceroy at Lima, to have anything whatsoever to do with such as we. Their attitude would seem to have ended the matter, but in the hope the Spaniards might have a change of heart and mind, we continued to lie off the town. We were still there on the morning of 25 April when we spied a small bark coming up from the southward. The general dispatched the pinnace, and others of our boats as well, out to meet the bark. However, the townspeople had sent men southward to stand on the hills and from there signal the approaching ship and warn her of the danger. Upon seeing the signals, and our boats too, the Spaniards ran their bark onto the shore about two miles from the town. Then they fled her. Our men boarded the prize but found so little of value in her that they left her and returned to us. The next morning we set fire to the big ship and sank one of the barks. The other bark, the better of the two, we kept and renamed the *George*. Having done that, we left Arica and resumed our voyage up the coast.

On 27 April we sighted a bark headed in the same direction as we were and, after a chase, we took her. Upon examining her men —there were five of them all told, a Greek pilot named George, three Spanish seamen and an old Fleming—we learned she was from Santiago which is not far from Quintero. We learned other things as well, some of which were of vast importance to us. For instance, the Spaniards were bearing letters regarding us to the viceroy at Lima. More, before leaving Santiago, each of the men had received the Sacrament; each, too, had been made to swear that if we should chance to take their ship they would destroy the letters.

Now it was a fact they had not willingly supplied all of this information to our general. First and in order that their tongues might be loosened, thumb screws, causing them extreme pain, were used upon the Spaniards. When they refused to talk, the general's attention swung to the old Fleming. He was prepared for hanging. He was even drawn up, not once but twice, by the neck until his feet cleared the deck. When let down, he was asked if he had anything to tell us. He said he had. He dared us to go ahead and hang him. Finally, one of the Spaniards weakened and told us all, whereupon we burned the bark and took the men with us.

On 3 May we entered a bay which stands in 13° 40′ south of the Equator. This bay has three little towns on its shores. It also has an island inhabited only by seals. We entered one of the towns, without resistance from its people, and took from it certain things such as hens, fruit, and bread, but other than those victuals there was nothing of value to tempt us. We lay there two days. Then we departed, leaving the *Content* as she was tarrying to take seals from an island. It was to be quite some time before she rejoined us.

Four days later, we spied a sail and gave chase. But she proved such a fleet craft we could not overtake her before night-fall and she escaped. During the long chase, the *Desire* and our new bark, the *George*, outdistanced the *Hugh Gallant* so that when the next morning broke, those of us who were in the *Hugh Gallant* could catch no sight of either the admiral or the bark. To be thus separated, caused us considerable worry. However, we could do no more than continue on course and place our trust in the Almighty, hoping He would, in His own good time, see all of our fleet reunited.

The following day, 11 May, we put into a bay which stands in 12° 40′ south and discovered that a river empties into the bay. We also took notice that a town lies on one side of the river. The town being there made us wonder if we should attempt to take on water because we had, in the *Gallant,* only eighteen men. But the scarcity of our water, and its brackishness [saltiness], decided us and we sent a boat ashore. The boat crew filled some butts without interference from the people, and while they were about it, one of the seamen took a short stroll. In doing so, he came upon a huge pile of at least 500 bags of meal which was covered only by some reeds. That night, we returned and made off with a goodly portion of the meal; later, it became a welcome addition to our victuals. We remained in the bay until the following afternoon. During that time, the people of the town tried to entice us onto the land by driving cattle down to the beach and signalling to us that we could have them simply by coming ashore. Instead, we weighed anchor and put out to sea.

On 13 May we came into a bay and saw a small bark, or pinnace, of five or six tons hauled up on the beach. We also saw several horsemen. But despite the fact we were being watched, we determined to wait until night and then take the bark for our own purposes. To that end eight of us, which number included the captain and myself, went ashore and managed, after great effort, to launch the prize. Then Captain Bruer and I attempted to take it, by ourselves, back to the ship. The effort very nearly cost us our lives. Without warning of any sort, it began to leak and to sink at one and the same time. To add to our alarm, in the darkness our own boat was nowhere to be seen. However, all ended happily—aside from our toil having gone for naught.

On 16 May, despite our having so few men in the *Hugh Gallant,* we took a great ship called the *Lewis* which was of the burden of 300 tons and was laden with timber and victuals. We took some of the victuals. Then we slashed her rigging, sank her boats, and let her go. The next day we came up with the admiral, finding to our great relief that the entire fleet was once more reunited. While we had been parted from the admiral two ships had been taken. These ships had been so richly laden with merchandise of various sorts that had we been able to get them to a civilized country such as England each would have been worth £20,000. As it was, only such things as we could use then and there were removed from them and, that done, their people were put ashore and the ships set afire.

On 20 May we entered the road of Paita, a sizable place lying in 5° and a tierce [one-third of a degree], or thereabouts, southward of the Equator. Directly we came to anchor, the general landed with seventy men. After a short skirmish with some men of the town, he drove them from it so that the streets of Paita were pretty much ours, particularly as the greater part of the inhabitants had also fled to the hills. Paita, though, was still not completely ours. In a strong, fort-like building a number of slaves as well as others of the meaner sort had been commanded, by the governor, to stay and resist us in any way possible. The general, rather than risk losses by assaulting this fort outright, decided he would first test the resolution of its defenders by having the barks fire a few pieces at it. One shot sufficed. The fort's defenders fled toward the hills as fast as they could. To make certain they, or the others who had previously run from the town, would not return to bother us, the general had us pursue them miles inland.

While we were about this, we came upon a place where the inhabitants of Paita had taken many of their belongings in the belief that they would be safe from us. In the entire assortment of items only one interested us: twenty-five pounds of silver. As we did not wish to burden ourselves with articles we could do without, we took only the silver. The town of Paita, though well built, neat, and clean, yielded us so little that, after we had searched it for valuables, we set it afire and went back to our ships. A bark which we had found riding in the harbour we also set ablaze. Then we departed.

On 25 May we arrived by the Island of Puna. Puna, which in size is somewhat like our own Isle of Wight, lies in the Gulf of Guayaquil and has a very good harbour. We would have liked to have gone directly into that harbour but a calm forced us to lie some distance offshore. As we lay there, a canoe, one we surmised had been sent to spy upon us, ventured too near and we captured it, and its occupant, an Indian. From this man, whom we examined closely, we learned many things to our advantage. First, in the harbour there lay a ship of 250 tons, all readied to be hauled onto the shore for refitting. On the land itself there was a grand house owned by the lord of the island and, besides this mansion, there were at least 200 lesser houses wherein lived the Indian people who are slaves, or near-slaves, to the lord. This lord—he is known as the cacique—is himself an Indian but a Christian one, who has built a great church to which he makes all of the people go.

More, though of Indian blood, this cacique has for his wife a Spanish woman of marvelous fairness and great beauty. This woman behaves in all ways as though she were queen of the island and the people are expected to treat her as such. Her feet scarce ever touch the ground. Even when she goes abroad to take the air, she is borne in a canopied litter by four slaves and attended by a number of ladies-in-waiting. Completing the procession, and acting as guards, is a troop of the best and the tallest men of Puna. None of this was bad tiding for us as it suggested there might be much of value to be had for the taking. Alas, our captive—he claimed he was a captain of the Indians—ended our high hopes: The cacique, he said, had been warned of our coming and had left the island and gone over to the safety of the mainland, taking with him his entire household and his valuables, which latter included, in coin alone, 100,000 crowns.

Notwithstanding this bad news, when the wind permitted we brought our ships into the harbour, burning a ship which we found lying there. Then we landed and rummaged through the grand house of the lord, finding very little in it, for, even as our captive had warned us, just about everything of value had been removed. We went back aboard and the general debated what next we should do. He questioned our prisoner still further, and more closely too, with the result the man admitted he knew the place on the mainland to where the cacique had taken his household—and his treasure. He also told us we might very easily take the place as it consisted of no more than four houses and had no defences of any kind. Having acquired this knowledge, our general, on 27 May, late in the day took a number of men, as well as the Indian who would act as a guide, and went to the mainland.

However, upon our coming to the spot where our captive told us we should land, we found four newly built and very large balsas [boats made from balsa wood]. The boats were unattended—but not empty. All four were laden with plantains, bags of meal, and other victuals. When our guide was asked if he knew anything about the balsas, he replied that he did not. This caused the general to warn him that lies could cost him his life. He then reminded the Indian that he had told us that the place where the lord had gone had only three or four houses. If this should prove untrue he would be hanged. The general then ordered the Indian to be tightly bound, and when that was done the general again asked him if he knew anything about the balsas. This time the fellow's tongue was loosened. He insisted he did not know from whence the balsas had come, but he had been told they were to bring sixty soldiers to join 100 who were already at a place called Guayaquil, a town about six leagues from the Island of Puna. The soldiers, he said, were at Guayaquil to guard three ships, belonging to the king of Spain, which were on the stocks being built. The captain of the place, having had news of us and being fearful we would try to destroy the ships, had requested the extra soldiers.

We could get no further information out of the Indian. But our general was not a whit discouraged by the knowledge that there might be three score Spanish soldiers at the place where the lord of Puna was supposed to be. Though it was by then night and very dark, we set out along a path which wound through the woods, doing so as quietly as we could. However, the cacique must have had men keeping watch along the shore. We arrived at the houses, only to find them empty. The people must have fled mere minutes before; food was still cooking by the fires. For all of our trouble, we had to content ourselves with taking some hens from their roosts. With that miserable loot, we returned to the ships.

Two days later the general went in the ship's boat to a small island lying just off Puna. There he had the good fortune to come upon the hiding place of various hangings from the great house which the lord had taken to the isle for safe keeping. Fashioned from the finest of Cordovan [Spanish] leather, the hangings were not without value. On the isle, as well, there was a considerable store of ship's cordage and iron nails. As we were in short supply of both items, they were brought away, thus proving that though the lord of Puna had thwarted us in most ways, in other ways we were the victors.

For instance, he and his people had had to leave behind them their flocks of sheep and goats, their horses and cattle, their hens, pigeons and turkeys. Besides their livestock, of course, were their gardens and fruit trees. The gardens had pumpkins, melons, cucumbers, radishes, rosemary, and thyme. The trees were producing oranges, limes, lemons, and divers other fruits. It was a land of such abundance we were loath to leave it so, instead, we lingered while we hauled the *Desire* out of the water and cleaned her hull, burnt her keel, and pitched and tarred her. Then, of course, we refloated her. During all of the days we had been working on her, we had been keeping what we thought was a sufficiently good watch against possible enemy attack. Alas, our diligence was not great enough, as was proven on the morning of 2 June.

That morning, just after daybreak, fewer than twenty of us were ashore, charged not only with keeping a lookout for the enemy but in fetching back fresh victuals. In pursuance of the latter task, some of us were gathering fruit from the trees while others were hunting down sheep and goats. As result, we became more separated and scattered than we should have. Of a sudden, there appeared fully 100 Spanish soldiers as well as a considerable number of Indians. They had landed—this we learned later—on the far side of the island during the night.

Two or three of our men, those who had been farthest afield, were set upon and slain. However, the shots that slew them warned the rest of us. We got into the houses and, thus sheltered, we defended ourselves stoutly for at least an hour. At the end of that time we decided on a bold move: We left the houses and fell back to the water's edge—only to discover that the pinnace in which we had come ashore, had been taken and burned by the Spaniards. This left us in a bad way indeed as we were forced to defend ourselves as best we could until such time as another boat from the ships could come to take us off. While we waited, there was fierce fighting, during which one of our men, a Zacharie Saxie, slew two Spaniards with his halberd [a combination pike and axe] alone before being killed by a shot through his heart.

Shortly after that, a boat arrived. But such was our haste to get into it, that we almost capsized it. Worse, a man named Robert Maddocke had his own snaphaunce [musket] discharge by accident and shoot him through the head, killing him. As a final misfortune, it was discovered that the boat simply could not take the lot of us. Therefore, four men, one of them myself, were left behind. We managed to get in among some rocks on a nearby cliff. There we defended ourselves with our pieces until a boat came to take us away. In this encounter we lost nine killed and three taken prisoner. The Spanish lost, in our estimation, more than forty dead.

That same day, bent on revenge, we went to the place where the king of Spain's ships were being built. It proved to be a town of some 300 houses and it was defended by, at very least, 100 Spanish soldiers and double that number of Indians, though the latter were armed only with bows. Despite this force which was mustered against us, seventy of us landed and, attacking with great fierceness, drove them from the town. With the place to ourselves, we set fire to the houses and the ships. We also did whatever damage we could to their fields and orchards. Then we returned to the harbour of Puna. The next day, ignoring the possibility of a Spanish attack, we began to do to the *Content* what we had done to the *Desire*. And while part of the company were working on the hull of the *Content*, others were repairing the damage done to our pinnace when the Spaniards had set it afire.

On 5 June we left the road of Puna and went northward to the Rio Dolce where we watered. In the mouth of the Rio Dolce we emptied the *Hugh Gallant* and sank her, for the good reason we no longer had the men to man her. We stayed by the river until 11 June. Before departing, we set ashore some Indians we had taken prisoner when first we came to the Island of Puna. The next day, 12 June, we crossed the Equator. For the remainder of June we held course steadily to the northward. Our progress was such that by 1 July a sighting revealed we were in 10°. More, to starboard and not over four leagues distant lay the coast of Nueva Espana [New Spain].

On 9 July we took a ship, a new one, of the burden of 120 tons which had, as its crew, seven men, one of them a skilled pilot named Michael Sancius who was familiar with the coast of New Spain. Our prize, though, had very little in her which could be called merchandise. However, we profited in that we stripped her of her sails, ropes and firewood. Then we set her afire, keeping her men. In particular we were anxious to have Sancius with us. He could be depended upon to guide us to watering places along the coast. It was from this same Sancius that we first heard of a great ship called the *Santa Anna*. Mark well the name as more will be heard of this ship.

The next day we took another ship, a bark. Taking her had been a stroke of good fortune indeed as our captive pilot had already, while being examined, informed us that this particular bark was one which had been sent along the coast to warn the towns, and the ships, against us. When we boarded her she was deserted. Her men, having recognized us for what we were, had taken to their boats and fled to the land. As she contained no goods to speak of, we set her afire to prevent the Spaniards making further use of her.

On 26 July we entered the mouth of the Copalita River and came to anchor in order to replenish our water. This river stands in 15° 40′ north. It also happens to be not more than two leagues distant from the town of Aguatulco [Guatulco]. Its nearness to the town caused us to that night put off in our pinnace with thirty men. At daybreak the following morning, we entered the road of Aguatulco, finding a bark, minus its crew, lying at anchor. We boarded the bark, which was laden with cacao nuts and indigo. The former is a nut somewhat like an almond which the people of the country both eat and make a drink from; the latter is a shrub used in the making of dye. When we had rummaged through the ship, we landed and set fire to over 100 houses in the town. Too, we fired both their church and their custom house. The custom house had in it 600 bags of indigo and 400 bags of cacao nuts. Each bag of indigo—it is really a shrub called anil—was worth forty crowns while a bag of the nuts ran to the value of ten crowns. We took very little from the custom house, except some boxes of balm which I came upon in a flasket, or long, narrow woven basket.

When we had spoiled the town, the captain of the ship came down to us with a flag of truce and, after Captain Havers had promised him a safe return, he came off with us in our pinnace to where our ships lay. Coming aboard, he talked at length with the general, but what was said I do not know. That night, the Spaniard was put back ashore. The following day, 28 July, we left the river, mostly because the tides would not allow us to fill our water butts properly with fresh water. We moved the ships into the road of Aguatulco. When night came, our general took thirty men and went into the woods. He and his company returned to us with a prisoner, a mestizo, which is the name given to one whose father is Spanish but whose mother is Indian. After the mestizo had been examined he was put ashore.

On 2 August, by which time we had finally managed to fill our water butts, we left Aguatulco and, holding course along the coast we passed by, without our knowing it, the town of Acapulco. Acapulco is a very important place as it is from there that the great galleons set forth for the Philippines. On 24 August the general, again taking thirty men, went in the pinnace to a place called Puerto de Natividad, as Sancius, our captive pilot, had said a small pearling ship, a pinnace really, worked out from there. When the general and his men arrived, it was only to find that the pearler was away at sea. However, it was learned by questioning the Indians of the place that a mulatto had recently arrived, by horse, from the south and was then sleeping in one of the houses. The man was taken and on him were found letters warning the coast against us. The letters were taken, the horse was slain, but the mulatto was allowed to go free.

On 26 August we came into the Bay of Santiago. A river flows into that bay so we took on water, as well as a quantity of plantains which we found growing along the river. Too, we cast our nets and took fish. Some of the men tried dragging for pearls and had some success. The Bay of Santiago is 19° 18′ north of the Equator. We departed 2 September. The following day the general and thirty men landed at the small town of Acatlin. Acatlin had thirty houses and a church; it is inhabited entirely by Indians. The Indians having fled at first sight of us, the general burned all of the houses, and the church as well. Then we went back aboard.

On 8 September we came into the road of Chaccala. Next morning before it was light, Captain Havers and forty men, and with Sancius as guide, left for a small village lying about two miles inland. To get there, we had to travel a most villainous path. Arriving at the place, we took three entire families prisoner, one Spanish, one Portuguese, one Indian, and brought them back with us to the ships. The three men were bound and kept as hostages so the women would bring us a supply of fruits such as plantains, lemons, limes, oranges, and pineapples. When we had sufficient store of the fruits, we let the Indian go. The white men we kept as we had a use for them, particularly the Spaniard who happened to be a carpenter. Leaving Chaccalla, we arrived on 12 September by an island which was well endowed with wood, fowls, seals, and a creature known as the iguano. The iguano is a four-footed serpent, very loathsome in appearance, but its flesh is excellent. We rode at anchor there until 17 September; then we left.

On 24 September we came into the road of Mazatlan which lies exactly on the Tropic of Cancer. Though there is a great river there, we had difficulty filling our butts with fresh water. Shoals kept us well offshore. However, we cast our nets and took many fish. We also found an abundance of fruit on the land. Departing from there on 27 September we ran to an island lying about a league, no more, to the northward of Mazatlan. There we trimmed the ships and rebuilt our pinnace. This island lies a mile offshore from the mainland. A Spanish prisoner named Domingo swam that mile, thus escaping from us. From the shore opposite us we were kept under constant watch by a considerable body of horsemen. Sancius informed us that the horsemen were there to discourage us from going into the country to despoil a town called Chiametla which, he said, is about eleven leagues distant from the coast.

While we were on that island, our fresh water became so diminished we feared we might have to go southward for as many as thirty leagues to replenish it, something we wished to avoid doing as we were keeping watch for a certain great ship we had been told about. However, we learned that among our prisoners was a man named Flores who had a gift from God. Flores, we were told, could find water even in a desert. Upon hearing this, our general, who had heard of such men before, commanded Flores to find us water. The man cast about for some time, making motions with his hands. Finally, he pointed to a certain spot. We dug where he indicated and, about three feet down, we came upon such an abundance of sweet water we could have taken 1,000 tons of it.

We left that island on 9 October holding such a course that on 14 October we fell in with the Cape St. Lucar [Lucas, on southern tip of Lower California], which cape reminds one more than a little of the Needles of our own Isle of Wight. Within the cape is a great bay, called by the Spaniards Aguada Segura, into which flows a fairsized river. We watered in the river's mouth, then lay off and on the cape, keeping watch for the certain ship. This cape, incidently, has another name: it is also known as the Headland of California. It stands in 23° 30′ north.

We were still lying off the cape on 4 November. On the morning of that date, at between seven and eight of the clock, the trumpeter of the *Desire* went aloft into the maintop. Scarcely was he up there than he gave a great shout of: "A sail! A sail!" The further good news he shouted down to us was that the sail belonged to a very great ship and that she was bearing in, from the westward, toward the cape. We prayed she was the galleon we had been lying in wait for: The *Santa Anna* of 700 tons, owned by the king of Spain and his admiral ship of the South Sea.

Immediately the trumpeter had cried down his glad tidings, divers others of the company, including even the master, were swarming aloft in order that they, too, might see the ship. There was a great deal of huzza-ing. The general allowed all of them their look. Then he commanded that both ships be made ready for battle and, too, that they be set on such a course as would bring them up with the *Santa Anna.* Thus began the chase that lasted for hours as the Spaniard showed us his heels and we gained but slowly on him.

It was past noon when we came up with them. And right away, we gave them a broadside of both our great and our small ordnance. Then we closed and tried to lay them aboard, even though we had no more than sixty men in our ship. But the Spaniards had prepared themselves for just such event. In their amidships, their waist if you will, they had put up fights, or barricades. On both poop and forecastle they had hung sails, as though they were curtains, so that not a man of them could we see. We were well aware, though, that there were more of them than there were of us, and that they were standing behind their fights and screens, waiting for us with swords, javelins, and even stones.

As we ranged up beside the *Santa Anna,* we made the discovery she was so mighty she towered over us. This greatly favoured the Spaniards as it allowed them to send a shower of rocks down upon both our heads and our decks. But disregarding their missiles, we cast our irons [iron hooks to hold the ships together] and a few of our men actually gained their deck. However, those few were so fiercely assailed that two were slain and five more wounded.

Very quickly we gave up the notion of taking the *Santa Anna* in that fashion. We disengaged and drew away. Then by trimming our sails, we came back and once more presented them with a broadside. This we could do as our ships, though tiny compared to theirs, were fleeter and handled better. Again and again we repeated the performance, each time raking the Spaniard, killing many of her men and maiming still more. With little damage to ourselves we were thoroughly worsting them, but their captain, who was a valiant man, refused to yield. Nor would he until more than five hours of fighting had gone by. Then with his ship so full of holes she was in grave danger of sinking, he put up a flag of truce.

In an exchange of words between the Spanish captain and our general, the captain asked only for mercy for his people. The goods in his ship we could have.

Our general straightaway promised them mercy—on condition they strike their sails and send certain persons aboard the *Desire.* This they consented to do. The sails of the *Santa Anna* came in and a boat was lowered so that their captain, their chief merchant, and their pilot could come over to our ship. When these three important personages had ascended the ladder and come over the rail, each, and in turn beginning with the chief merchant, knelt and kissed the general's feet. Each begged for mercy and pardon. Our general promised them good usage, providing of course, that they resist us in no way and do, within reason, anything we asked them to do. To these demands they agreed.

The terms settled, our general at once asked the captain and the pilot of the *Santa Anna* to provide him with a list of the goods she carried. The list having been given, we learned she was richly laden with silks, satins, damasks, perfumes, and other valuable items of merchandise. She was well supplied with victuals. Lastly, she had in her strongbox 122,000 pesos of gold!

We took this great ship into the harbour of Puerto Segura, the better to remove from her the things we wished to have. Meantime, we set ashore all of her people—they numbered 190—excepting the captain, the pilot, and a few others. Our general went to great lengths to see that the people who had been placed ashore should suffer as little as possible. First, they were put by a river so they would have fresh water. They were given a generous supply of victuals, tents to protect them from the sun, and arms so they could hunt the fowls, hares, and rabbits which abound in the region. Last, the general gave them planks sufficient to build themselves a bark so that they might, in time, effect their own rescue.

Their comfort seen to, we fell to looting the *Santa Anna,* giving, as we did so, to each man of the company his fair share of the treasure. However, this led to the men of the *Content* rising up in mutiny because, they said, they were not receiving their just portions. The general convinced them they were, and they became pacified—after a fashion. By 17 November our task was nearing completion. That being so and, too, as it happened to be the anniversary of our Queen's coronation, the general ordered us to celebrate by firing off all of our ordnance. That night, he again had us fire them. He also had fireworks which made for a very great display in the darkness. Our Spanish prisoners were amazed as it is not their custom to celebrate in such a way or manner.

The following day our general began making final preparations for our departure. The first thing he did, he discharged the captain of the *Santa Anna* giving him, as he did so, a rather royal reward. He also supplied him with pieces, shot, powder, shields, and other items in such quantity as should guarantee the safety of his people against attack by Indians. Then and because we were short-handed, he took into the *Desire* two good lads who had been born in Japan. One of these was named Christopher and was about twenty years old; the other was called Cosmus and he was seventeen. He also took three boys who were natives of the isles of Manila [Philippines]. Their ages were fifteen, thirteen, and nine. The youngest, a mere child, is today servant to the Countess of Essex. Besides those five, we took three others: A Portuguese named Roderigo, a Negro, and a Spaniard called Ersola. The Portuguese and the Negro would, we hoped, act as interpreters for us once we reached the islands we would be heading for. Ersola, the Spaniard, was the greatest of the catch. As a pilot, he had made various voyages between Acapulco and the Ladrones [now, Mariana Islands, east of the Philippines], therefore he could be prevailed upon to guide us to such isles as would provide us with fresh water, plantains, potatoes, and other necessities.

Our preparations for departure completed, the general ordered us to set fire to the *Santa Anna.* When she was well ablaze, we fired a gun, hoisted our sails, and put to sea at about three of the clock in the afternoon of 19 November. Joyfully and with a fair breeze, we soon cleared the harbour. The *Content,* though, for reasons unknown to us, lagged and did not follow us to sea. We thought nothing of it. Something had detained her, but she would overtake us shortly. Instead, and to our very great sorrow, we never saw her again. What fate befell her, God only knows.

. . .

The remainder of the trip was relatively uneventful with the exception of the death of Captain Havers on the 21 February 1588 of "the pestilent ague." On 9 September, "after surviving a terrible storm which carried away the most of our sails," the ships sailed into Plymouth harbour.

As regards the *Santa Anna,* the elements were more kindly than Thomas Cavendish. Scarcely was Cavendish clear of the harbour than a fierce gale, accompanied by torrential rains, struck. The gale drove the still-burning *Santa Anna* ashore, where the marooned Spaniards quickly seized the opportunity this gave them to save what they could of the ship. Swarming back aboard, they began to fight the fire. Aided by the torrential rain they quickly put it out. Later they patched the ship sufficiently to sail her to the Mexican coast and safety.

One can also wonder if the violent storm which struck right after Cavendish left the harbour of Puerto Segura did not have some bearing on the disappearance of the *Content.* Cavendish made no attempt to go back and search for the missing ship. Centuries later the bones of an European ship were found on one of the Hawaiian Islands. Some hold the theory that the wreck was that of the *Content.*

Tracing the route taken by Cavendish as he rounded the world is not very difficult. Credit for this must go to Master Pretty for faithfully recording the latitudes of the various places they called at. As Drake had done before him, Cavendish and his men went first to the Barbary coast of Africa, sailing along it until they came to the Rio de Oro. From the Rio de Oro they sailed to Sierra Leone, by which time it is believed that Cavendish's men were suffering from scurvy. However, fresh foods improved their health as the fleet lingered to take on a complete supply of wood and water. Leaving Sierra Leone they proceeded to Cape Verdes Islands, from where they set course for South America.

Cavendish had with him charts made by Drake after his own voyage around the world. He also had, among his company, men who had been with Drake. Therefore he knew fairly well what to expect from the coast, or coasts, of South America.

Cavendish's ships entered Port Desire on 17 December according to Pretty. Other writers have expressed the opinion that they came to Port Desire much sooner. They left there, says Pretty, on 28 December, putting into the Strait of Magellan on 6 January.

Cavendish, as he no doubt expected, found the pickings lean along the western coast of South America. Drake had taught the Spaniards a not-to-be-forgotten lesson. When Cavendish arrived, Spanish ships were carrying ordnance; the larger centres of population were fortified. That being the case, there was no boldly sailing into such places as Valparaiso or Callao. In fact, the Spaniards were so constantly alert, Cavendish could scarcely land in search of water, even in out-of-the-way places, without being confronted by a host of armed men. The truth is, had Cavendish not learned about the treasure ship *Santa Anna,* the entire voyage would have been a financial failure.

Upon leaving lower California, Cavendish and his men had a fast passage across the Pacific. In forty-five days they sighted Guam, one of the Marianas. The Spanish, for reasons which soon became evident to Cavendish, called these islands the Islands of Thieves. The part of the Philippines first sighted by Cavendish, the cape referred to as Cabo del Spirito Santa (Cape of the Holy

Spirit), stands on the northwest corner of Samar. From there, and because he had better charts than Drake had had, Cavendish worked his way right through the Philippines, rather than going completely around them as Drake had done.

From the Philippines, Cavendish headed for the strait separating Java and Sumatra. They were on their way home. On 16 March they departed Java; on 8 June they reached St. Helene in the Atlantic. As no mention is made of their landing anywhere in between, this can only mean that they were at sea for eighty-four days. On 9 September Cavendish sailed into Plymouth harbour.

Shortly after, the *Desire* left Plymouth and proceeded to London where it was given a state welcome. For the thousands of cheering Londoners, the *Desire* put on a brave show. Cavendish had her topmasts wrapped in what looked like cloth of gold—but was really a material woven from silkgrass which the natives of the east use for sails. His seamen were still more eye-catching in appearance. They were decked out in the then-priceless fabrics: silks, brocades and satins. Ordinarily, such garments were worn only by kings and princes. It is said, and probably with truth, that the whole of England applauded when Cavendish knelt and was knighted by the Queen.

Cavendish went around the world in two years and fifty days. Magellan's surviving ship took three years and one month. Drake did it in two years, ten months and eleven days.

The last voyage of

Thomas Cavendish

as told by Master John Janes

The 26 August 1591, we departed Plymouth in our fleet of three tall ships and two barks: the *Galeon,* into which went our general, Master Cavendish, was our admiral ship; the *Roebucke* with Master Cocke as captain was vice admiral. The *Desire* commanded by Master John Davis (it was for his sake I went on this voyage) was the rear admiral. Besides the above-mentioned ships, there were two barks, one of which was the *Black Pinnace,* while the other belonged to Master Adrian Gilbert and had for its captain Master Randolph Cotton.

On 29 November we fell in with the Bay of Salvador on the coast of Brazil, twelve leagues to the northward of Cabo Frio [near Rio de Janeiro], which lies 23° south of the Equator. There we were becalmed for three days. However, during that time we took a bark, bound for the River Plate, which had in her sugar, haberdashery goods, and Negro slaves. We persuaded the master of this prize to pilot us to the Isle of Placentia, lying thirty leagues to the westward of Cabo Frio and, therefore, close to the mouth of the River January. Arriving at the isle on 5 December, we rifled six or seven houses belonging to the Portuguese and remained there until 11 December. Then we left. Three days later we were by the Isle of San Sebastion. Our admiral ship, the *Galeon,* and the two barks cast their anchors and stayed at San Sebastion. Not so the *Roebucke* and *Desire.* Our general gave orders to Captains Cocke and Davis that they should proceed, at once, to the town of Santos with the view of taking it so that our entire fleet might be revictualled from supplies found there.

It was the evening of 15 December when we anchored *Desire* and *Roebucke* off the bar of San Sebastion. Two boats, one from each ship, were immediately sent away, but during the darkness they became separated, with the *Roebucke*'s boat falling far behind the *Desire*'s, the one I was in. Captain Davis, though, did not allow this to deter us. Arriving by the town at about nine of the clock in the morning, we landed twenty-four armed gentlemen and had the rare good fortune to find most all of the townspeople at Mass. Surrounding the church, we held the people captive all that day. We had, in our opinion, done our part and more. We relied upon Captain Cocke, whom our general had entrusted with the command of the venture, to come up and do what should be done: Take possession of all the victuals in the town of Santos.

Captain Cocke did finally come up. But such was his negligence that, while his men were engaged in all sorts of matters which suited their fancy, Indians were to be seen carrying, in plain sight, from the town whatsoever they chose. Thus it was that, due to Captain Cocke's lack of diligence, the Indians, and not his men, stripped Santos bare of victuals. As result, our troubles in taking the place went for naught.

As there seemed no further point in keeping the townspeople prisoner, we let them leave the church—all except four old men. Those four we kept, in the hope we could use them as pawns to force the inhabitants of the town to give us the things we needed. With our prisoners we returned to the ships. Ten days later, the general himself went to Santos. But to our disappointment, the townspeople would not pay ransom in order to get their old men back. Truth is, they refused to deal with us in any way whatsoever, even though we lay off their town until 22 January. In the finish, we departed in much worse state than when we arrived. In anger, we entered the town of St. Vincent which lies not far from Santos and burned it. Then we held course toward the Strait of Magellan.

On 7 February there was a great storm, which continued on well into the next day and scattered the fleet so that the ships lost sight of each other. Our ship, the *Desire,* being by herself and Captain Davis having received no specific instructions from the general on what action to take during such an extremity, conferred with the ship's master, who was an honest and sufficient fellow, as to what should be done. Between them, they decided we should resume course to the southward, holding it until we arrived at Port

Desire in latitude 48°. Both were of the opinion that the general would head for there himself, as it is the port where he lingered for a time during his first voyage.

In sailing toward Port Desire, we met up with the *Roebucke.* When within hailing distance, their captain told us they were in great difficulty, being low on victuals and having lost their ship's boat during the tempest. Captain Davis listened to the woeful tale, then ordered a boat hoist out so he could go over to the *Roebucke.* He returned, satisfied that both ship and company were in desperate case. From then on, we kept the *Roebucke* close by us in order that she might not be lost. She was still in consort with us when we entered Port Desire, safely, on 6 March. On 16 March the *Black Pinnace* appeared. From her company we learned that the bark of Master Gilbert had given over the venture and returned to England—after having placed her captain, Master Cotton, aboard the *Black Pinnace,* bereft of all his belongings other than the clothing he wore. Very soon Captain Cotton came over to the *Desire* so he could be with his old friend, Captain Davis. He remained with us from then on.

Two days later the admiral ship, the *Galeon,* arrived, though Master Cavendish was not with her. He came soon afterwards in a small boat he had built while at sea because all of their other boats, a longboat, a light-horseman, and a pinnace, which pinnace had been put together at Santos, had all been lost during the storm. Master Cavendish came directly to the *Desire,* for the express purpose of unburdening himself, into the ears of Captain Davis, of a multitude of grievances he held against the men of the *Galeon.* He would, he vowed, remain from then on on the *Desire.* We took no delight in hearing the general speak so harshly of our friends on the *Galeon.* For our own part, we had always found them faithful and honest.

On 20 March we put out of Port Desire. From then until 8 April, we were constantly punished by one great storm after another. Despite the storms, though, on the above-mentioned date we were off the entrance to the Strait of Magellan. On 14 April we passed through what is termed the first strait; by 16 April we had gone forward another ten leagues, passing through the second strait. Two days later we doubled Cape Froward. This cape—it lies in 53° 30′—is the most southerly point of Magellan's strait. During the next three days we managed to get only four leagues beyond Cape Froward. Then the fury of the weather had us seeking shelter in a small cove on the southern side of the strait. In that cove we lay for the remainder of April and, until 15 May, not once daring to put forth. Storm followed storm, each of them a wild gale bringing rain, sleet and snow. During those days, as we were woefully short on victuals, we subsisted mainly on mussels and seaweed. The seamen, many of whom lacked sufficient clothing to properly cover their bodies, suffered beyond description. Various of them died.

During this extremity, a most uncharitable deed was done. All of the sick who were aboard the *Galeon* were put ashore, to fend for themselves, in the woods. Naturally, for indeed men in full health could not have survived the snow, the cold, and the hunger, all of the men placed ashore soon died. And while this most shameful of acts was being performed, the general remained safely, and in some comfort, aboard the *Desire*.

At the height of our difficulties and uncertainties, the general talked at great length with our captain, seeking his advice, as Captain Davis is a man who has had much experience in Arctic regions, having made no fewer than three voyages to the northwest. Captain Davis gave as his opinion that the weather would, and before too long, improve. Captain Davis' advice was not taken. Instead, the general called the company together and told them he intended to quit the Strait of Magellan and return to the Atlantic. Once back on the eastern side of the strait, he said, we would have two choices. The first of these was that we could return up the coast of Brazil. The second, and the one he himself favoured the most, was that we sail for New Spain by way of Cape Buena Esperanza [Cape of Good Hope, at the tip of South Africa].

Upon hearing this, various members of the company brought forth a number of reasons why we should still try to reach the South Sea by way of the Strait of Magellan. They reminded the general that we had not, as of then, been in the strait for any great length of time. What was more, we were not above, at very most, forty leagues from its western entrance. In their opinion we should persist in going forward. The general, despite their arguments, was all for returning to the eastward and departing for Cape of Good Hope.

When the meeting was over and Captain Davis had the general to himself aboard the *Desire,* he once again begged Master Cavendish to change his mind, pointing out to him how woefully lacking we were in both supplies and men for such a long voyage as was proposed. His own ship, our captain said, was without sails and cordage, aside from that which was then on the masts and yards. We were the next thing to being completely out of victuals. True, we had in our company seventy-five persons. But no more than fifteen of those were mariners and in sufficient health to work the ship. The others, he reminded the general, were gentlemen, servants, and artificers. Captain Davis presented these facts quite vigorously, not alone to Master Cavendish but to Captain Cocke as well. However, and despite a petition drawn up and duly signed by the principal persons of the entire company, the general was still for our returning back through the strait. But his mind had been changed in one respect. He would not, he said, sail for New Spain by way of Africa. Instead, he would return up the coast of Brazil, to Santos. He then made solemn promise to our Captain Davis that, if his ships could be revictualled, he would return to the strait and carry on with the venture as previously planned.

On 15 May we set sail—but the general was no longer with us on the *Desire.* He was back aboard the *Galeon.* Our return through the strait was accomplished without great difficulty. But not, alas, without mishap. Off Cape Froward our only ship's boat, which we had been dragging astern, struck on a rock during the darkness of the night. It split and sank. Though when it came light, we managed to get the splintered craft up and aboard in the hope of later rebuilding it, all of its oars were lost. Three days later, on 18 May, we were free of the strait. By 20 May we were athwart Port Desire but well to sea of it. That night we again became separated from our admiral ship, the *Galeon.* When, in the morning, we could not sight it we reasoned that it had suffered some sort of mishap and, in consequence, had put into Port Desire in order that the ship might be repaired at the same time the Company refreshed themselves.

Our Captain Davis who, as of the moment, was unsure in his mind as to what to do, called the company together and desired an expression of opinions. Most everyone said they thought the general had taken the *Galeon* into Port Desire. But when the question was put as to whether we should follow him there, the master rose and spoke at great length. As he was a man of good judgement, honest, and an excellent seaman, we listened. In forceful words he told us we would be placing ourselves in grave danger should we attempt to go to Port Desire. In particular, he pointed to the fact we lacked a ship's boat, a necessity on account of the strong tides and currents at Port Desire. When he had spoken thus, the idea of our going to Port Desire was given over, even though the general, and the *Galeon*, might be there. Instead, we hoisted sail and held on course toward Santos. Very shortly, though, we came up with the *Black Pinnace* which, like ourselves, had become separated from the fleet during the darkness.

Upon our closing with the *Black Pinnace* and holding conversation with her company, we were informed that they were in a most miserable state. However, they were fortunate in having one thing we lacked: a ship's boat. If the ships stayed by each other one boat could serve both. That being so, the captains and the masters, after conferring, decided we should return to Port Desire.

We came into Port Desire on 26 May. To our vast disappointment, the general was not there. However, we had a stroke of good fortune; we found a very quiet road where we moored the ships. Then upon our going ashore in the *Black Pinnace*'s boat, good fortune was again our companion. We discovered a very good, and ample, pool of sweet water. Because when we had first been at Port Desire, we had had great difficulty supplying the ships with fresh water, we concluded that God, in His infinite mercy, had guided us to the pool. Nor did He confine his blessings to just those two things. At the ebb of the tide, mussels could be had in abundance. And besides the mussels, God sent about our ships vast schools of smelts. We caught them at will with hooks fashioned from pins. What with mussels and smelts, and other things as well, we were never hungry while we were at that place. The few regular ship's victuals we still had we kept and scarcely touched.

While we were renewing our bodies, Captain Davis and the master debated what should be done about the ship, as it was in a woeful state of disrepair. In their estimation it would require a month at least to make the *Desire* anything like seaworthy. And to accomplish this, we would have to set up upon the land a forge, and make charcoal, so that bolts, spikes, and nails could be fashioned. We were completely out of all of those necessary items. Besides the worries over refitting the ship, there still remained the question of how to inform the general, not alone of what we were doing, but of our whereabouts.

After a great deal of consultation, it was decided that into the *Black Pinnace* should go the men who were most in health, and what victuals we could spare. Then the *Black Pinnace* would go northward, rejoin the general, and assure him we would be in Port Desire, waiting for him when he again headed southward for the strait. The captain and the master of the *Black Pinnace,* both of them the general's men, were well satisfied with this arrangement.

All would have gone as planned—had it not been that we had, in our ship, two pestilent fellows: Charles Parker and Edward Smith. When that precious pair heard of what was proposed, they utterly mistrusted the whole idea. In secret, they went among the men of both companies, whispering that Captain Davis and the master of the *Desire* were men without either mercy or charity who would, if it suited their purpose, leave men in the country to be devoured by the cannibals. So persuasive were the tongues of the two villains that many men, and from both companies, joined them in a plot to murder Captain Davis, the master, myself, and various others whom they judged to be loyal to us. So far did the vile conspiracy develop that marks were made on the wall of Captain Davis' cabin. The marks were made so that men with muskets would know where to aim, and shoot, through the wall in order that the captain might be killed by the bullets. There were also, though this I realize is quite beyond belief, silver bullets made. These special bullets would be employed to execute the captain, should other means fail.

The plot might well have succeeded had not the boatswain of the *Desire* learned of it. He revealed it to the master. The master told the captain. Captain Davis, taking into consideration the hardships the men had endured, and the perils they were still in, weighed everything carefully—then decided to be lenient toward the conspirators. In the firm belief that he could, by courteous means, pacify them and cool their anger, he called all of them together. He then, in soft and reasonable words, explained to them as fully as he could precisely why it was proposed to send the

Black Pinnace northward to rejoin the general. More, he said, was involved than merely letting the general know of our plans and whereabouts. The pinnace belonged with the main fleet as the larger ships, the *Roebucke* and the *Galeon,* would be greatly hindered by their size from venturing close in to shore. As result, many an opportunity of taking things might be lost. A shallow-draught vessel such as the *Black Pinnace* was a necessity to the general.

The men, though, remained both unconvinced and sullen. Voicing their anger in words, they began shouting and cursing and demanding that the ships remain together, and that if one ship went northward the other should also go. But despite their unreasonable mood and their unseemly behaviour, Captain Davis remained patient. In quiet words, he asked them to remember that they were Christians, requesting of them that they show themselves as such. Going on from there, he reminded them that God, in His mercy, had but recently come to their assistance. He had guided them into the good road where the ships were then lying; He had provided them with an abundance of sweet water, mussels, and smelts. The captain proceeded to warn the men that by showing their ingratitude by blaspheming they were inviting sharp punishment from the same Lord who was sustaining them. This gentle speech of the captain, during the course of which he offered forgiveness to all including Parker and Smith, quietened matters. However, it was agreed, by motion and a large majority, that the ships should not separate but that both should continue to lie in Port Desire until the general returned.

Captain Davis bowed to the motion. He straightaway, though, presented to the company a motion of his own. The motion, in written form and signed, would show that neither he, Captain Davis, nor for that matter any of the company, was to blame for our becoming separated from the general. The company approved of the motion.

. . .

We then began to work for our very lives. Ashore, we built a smith's forge and a coalpit. We also made charcoal for use in the said forge, so that soon the smith was hard at work making nails, bolts, and spikes from scraps of iron. While he was doing that, others of us were making rope from pieces of our cable. The carpenters were hard at it rebuilding our boat which had suffered such damage back in the strait. The remainder of the company, the few not engaged in the above-mentioned activities, were charged with keeping us supplied with fresh victuals in the form of mussels, smelts, seals, and penguins. The seals and the penguins had to be taken from a group of small isles lying about three leagues from the road where the ships were. At that time of the year penguins in great abundance come to the isles to breed.

Once we had the *Black Pinnace*—we had gone directly to work upon her—in condition for putting to sea, our Captain Davis reached an agreement with her captain. It was this: The *Black Pinnace* would, when necessary, go to the isles in order to bring back seals and penguins which would be shared with the company of the *Desire*. In return, men from our company would assist in work which still had to be done on the smaller ship. We rather begrudged the time spent by men going and returning from the isles. But we simply had to have the meat from the seals and the penguins. True it is that mussels and smelts were plentiful, but there were times, especially just before and after the springtides, when the mussels were denied us.

Under those conditions, we remained in the road of Port Desire until we were into the month of August. Each day we spent there we had lookouts posted upon the hills. The lookouts were charged with keeping a constant watch for the return of the general. But with each passing day, our hopes of sighting the other ships waned. That being so, Captain Davis and our master fell to wondering if perhaps the general had gone directly to the strait without bothering to call at Port Desire. They finally came around to deciding that we should go into the strait ourselves, their reasoning being that if the other ships were already there we would stand at least an equal chance of finding them as we did by keeping watch from the hills near Port Desire. Thinking along the same lines, they concluded that if the ships had still not gone into the strait, we would be certain to sight them when they did as the strait, throughout most of its length, is so narrow a ship could not possibly pass us without being sighted.

In order that there might be no misunderstandings, Captain Davis and the master conferred with the captain and the master of the *Black Pinnace.* They agreed we should re-enter the strait so, upon 6 August, we set sail and went to the penguin isle. There we landed and slew enough of the seals to fill twenty hogsheads. We would have taken more but for one reason: We had run ourselves out of salt. Without being salted, the meat would spoil very quickly.

On 7 August we left the penguin isle and shaped course for the strait. On 9 August we had a severe storm which had us lying ahull and, speaking of lying ahull, we spent much of our time with all of our sails in. They were so weak and rotted we durst not put them out even in a brisk wind. On that occasion we drove, under bare poles, for the space of five days. Then on 14 August we were driven in among certain islands. We most firmly believe that these islands had never before been seen by civilized man. No chart shows them. No relation or narrative makes mention of them. In position, they lie about fifty leagues eastward of the mainland and are somewhat northerly of the Strait of Magellan [Falkland Islands].

Once in the shelter of these islands, it pleased God to have the winds cease. When they returned, which was not long after, they were from out of the east and gentle, enabling us to once more set course for the strait.

On 18 August we fell in with the cape at the entrance to the strait. Though there was fog, we continued on course so that, by evening, we were a full ten leagues to westward of the cape. The next day, 19 August, we passed through the first strait and the second strait as well. Two days later we rounded Cape Froward. The following day, 22 August, we anchored in Savage Cove, naming it that ourselves because we found many savages there. These people, despite the great cold, go naked and live in the woods like satyrs [mythical woodland beasts]. They paint their bodies and, wild as deer, will flee from you, not letting you get near them. However, we learned that they are men of enormous strength when, from an incredible distance, they hurled stones at us. Some of the stones weighed as much as three and even four pounds.

We departed from that particular cove on the morning of 24 August. In the afternoon of the same day we arrived at the northwest reach of the strait; the following day we anchored in a cove which is not above fourteen leagues in distance from the South Sea. There, we decided we would wait for the general as the strait, at that point, is not over a league in width. A ship could not possibly pass us without being seen. We lay in the cove for a fortnight, during all of which time the weather was of a most wintry nature. Our victuals ran low. The seal meat we thought we had cured went bad and began to stink most vilely. Various of our seamen, those lacking the proper clothing to protect them from the cold, died.

The distress of the company caused Captain Davis and the master such concern, that they decided we should remain no longer in the strait. It was their opinion we should proceed into the South Sea and then work northward along the coast until we arrived in a warmer clime. It was proposed we should go to the Isle of Santa Maria in 37° 15′ of south latitude. There, fresh victuals could be had and we would not be suffering from the cold while we waited for the general to come up. To that end, we departed from the cove on 13 September and by evening we were within sight of the South Sea. But the next day a strong westerly gale had us returning back into the strait for as much as three leagues in order to find shelter.

When the gale subsided we again put forth and, on this occasion, we got as many as eight, or probably even ten leagues into the South Sea. Once again, though, a furious gale, from the northwest this time, drove us back into the strait. This should not have happened, nor would we have let it happen, but for the bad state of our sails. The least bit of wind had us taking them in for fear they would blow out on us. Once more, we sought out the cove we had been in and came to anchor. This time, though, even the cove failed to give us sufficient shelter. The weather became so violent one of our cables—we had but two to begin with—broke and we lost an anchor. However, it pleased God to allow us to use our tackles, halyards, sheets, and other ropes and with them moor our ship to trees along the shore. The ship safe, we laboured mightily to recover our anchor. We failed, first, because it lay very deep and second—this was supposition on our part—because it was sunk well into ooze at the bottom.

The loss of the anchor left us with but one other, and it had a broken fluke, while for cables we had a single, very old one, which had already been spliced in two places. Nevertheless, we had to make do with them and so we used them. How next to worthless the cable was became evident when, on 1 October, we loosed the moorings and brought in our poor-affair of an anchor. The cable had given way until but a single strand of it remained.

We did not immediately put out our sails. We couldn't. Too much of our rigging ropes had been stripped for use in mooring. We had, therefore, to tow the *Desire* out of the cove. Once out into the channel, we worked for our very lives at getting the sheets, halyards and other lines and ropes back into place so we could make sail.

While we were hard at those tasks, arguments arose as to what we should do. A part of the company were loud in declaring we should return to Port Desire; the other part were as equally determined that we should stand by the captain and the master and, once more, continue on into the South Sea. The discord caused Captain Davis to speak in the following manner to the master, who, though this has not been previously mentioned, accompanied the general, Master Cavendish, on his first voyage:

"Master, you see what dire extremities we find ourselves in. There is great discontent among the men. Many are saying they doubt the truth of what you have told them regarding the comforts which will be ours should we succeed in clearing the strait and working northward along the coast. They say we are persisting chiefly out of our love and loyalty to the general. For mine own part, I admit this to be so. I first entered into this action because of my love and respect for the general. In doing so, I chose between him and others. That is truth. Coming on this voyage has cost me some of my best friends back in England. But no matter, I am still, if it pleases God, willing to proceed with the venture. However, I realize we are nearing the limits of both our resources and our endurance. I therefore, in Christian charity, entreat you to forgive me if you believe I have ever, in any way, treated you unjustly or unkindly. Second, I would rather hear you pray for the general than use harsh speeches against him. The state we now find ourselves in is not the fault of the general. More likely it is due our own offences against the Lord, as it would most certainly appear we are being punished by Him.

"In our present sad state, we should forgive one another all past grievances, be reconciled and practice love and charity in the hope that we may, if not in this world then in the next, find favour with the Almighty. And now, good master, as you have been on this voyage before, I charge you to go stand before the entire company. Speak to them, satisfy them that you have spoken the truth only about what we might expect if we continue on the voyage. There are other men in the company who were also with the general on his first voyage. Make those men come forward and, without fear of punishment, do one of two things: Bear you out or call you liar."

When the captain had finished, the master replied:

"Captain, your request is reasonable. I do not believe I have ever given you cause to doubt my love, my loyalty, to either my general or to you. You know, too, the anguish that has been mine at our losing the general. I would beg you to recall that, the night it occurred, I was sick abed. My mate was standing the watch. Had I been up and about it may not have happened, though of that we have no proof. When first I became a part of this venture, the general commanded me to follow and carry out each and every order given to me by yourself. If it is now your wish to return through the strait, I will do as you say. But it is my own opinion we should proceed. By doing so, I honestly believe we will have a better chance of surviving. Should we once get well into the South Sea, I swear I can, and before too long, bring you to an isle aswarm with penguins. They should sustain us until we reach the Isle of Santa Maria. Once there, we can have whatever we wish in the way of victuals: wheat, pork, meal, roots. Besides, when we reach the Isle of Santa Maria we will stand an excellent chance of meeting with, and taking, Spanish ships, for many of them ply along the coasts of Chili and Peru. On the other hand, if we return through the strait, I fear that little else than death awaits us."

The master then, and as directed, went before the company and spoke to them. When he was finished, men who had been with the general on his first voyage, came forward and confirmed the truth of the master's words. The grumbling ceased. It was decided, and by all, that we should continue with the voyage.

On 2 October we once again put into the South Sea, making such progress that by evening we were well clear of the land. Then with the coming of night there came also a furious wind from out the west-northwest. We were, once more, in great doubt as to what to do. We durst not put back into the strait for lack of a decent cable. Nor could we put out our sails for that or any other purpose. We knew, and knew well, they were so rotted the wind would have made shreds of them. While we were debating, and praying, the *Black Pinnace* came up close to us and told us they were in grave distress. Their ropes, they said, were breaking and failing them and they did not know what to do. We could not, alas, assist them in any way. We could not, at the moment, even help ourselves. We were expecting to be driven ashore to founder.

On 4 October the storm was still with us and still furious. Had we been well away from land there would have been no problem. We would have lain ahull and let the ship drive. But the wind's direction and the closeness of the shore forbid our doing that. Instead, we had to keep out a bit of sail so we could work the ship, and keep her clear of the land. While we were thus engaged in saving the *Desire*, downwind and to the northward of us, we could see the *Black Pinnace*. She, we noticed, was doing precisely as we were doing. But of a sudden, we saw that her company had taken in the rag of sail they had had out. They were letting the ship drive. We knew the *Pinnace* had suffered some grave misfortune, probably she had sprung a great leak. The wind and the seas prevented our going to their assistance. This I can say: She was still afloat when darkness fell. But we never saw her again.

The next day, 5 October, the storm was still very much with us, and we were labouring, as was usual, at keeping the ship clear of the land. Under her foresail only, we were succeeding. But then, and without warning, that sail split from top to bottom. It called for quick work on our part. While the wind tore at us, and the rain and the sleet pelted us, we salvaged what we could of the sail. Then the master had us remove the mizzen and take it forward and place it where the foresail had been. He also had us remove the spritsail from its yard and bring it inboard—so it could be used to repair the torn foresail. All of those tasks were performed while seas were running mountainously high.

On 10 October we were in a most miserable state. The weather was thick and dark. Most all of us had resigned ourselves to dying. Even Captain Davis had lost heart, and was seated in his cabin so cold he scarce could move a joint. In the hope of cheering him somewhat, I took him some wine and had him drink it. When he had, he felt better and then, for the ease of his conscience, he spoke of various things which had gone before. He concluded by appealing to the Lord in these words:

"Oh most glorious God, whose Power is such that the matters of the mightiest of men are of small moment, I humbly beseech Thee that the intolerable burden of my sins may, through the Blood of Jesus Christ, be taken from me. Oh Lord, I prithee to end now our suffering and our lives. Or, if it be Thy will that we survive, then hasten to show us some sign of Thy love. Amen."

Having ceased praying, he asked me not to make known to any of the company the unbearable grief and anguish that was his. It would, he said, only further dishearten them. However, and even while I was still with him, the Lord caused the clouds to part and the sun shone clear. Immediately, both he and the master busied themselves with observing the elevation of the Pole Antartica [South Pole], so that they might know what course we should set in order to re-enter the Strait of Magellan. Captain Davis, and the master too, were so revived in spirit that they spoke words of encouragement to all and, by so doing, had every man rejoicing as though our deliverance was already something assured us by the Almighty.

The mood of hopefulness remained to some extent with us and the following day we sighted Cape Deseado on the south shore of the entrance to the strait. When first seen, the cape was some two leagues to leeward of us, which meant that were we to enter the strait we would have to double the cape. This our master, taking into consideration the wind and the sad state of our sails and rigging, was in grave doubt we could do. When he expressed his fears to Captain Davis, the captain answered him in these words: "Double it we must. And no later than noon of this day, or we die. Loose then the sails, master. We will place our trust in them and in the Lord."

The master who, as I have mentioned before, was a man of spirit and dutiful too, immediately had the sails put out. But within the half hour the footrope of the foresail broke, leaving nothing to hold the sail but the eyelets. When this misfortune occurred our ship was being punished unmercifully. Time and again we had been pooped, meaning that great waves had broken over our stern, with the water actually flying into the sails. We feared the weight of that water would rend the sails, leaving them useless. To add to our fears, we could see we stood small chance of rounding the cape. Instead, we were within a half mile of the rocks and being driven closer. The surf was already rebounding off the ship's side. It was then that the master veered the mainsheet somewhat. Whether as result of the master's doing this, or some current or, what is the likeliest of all, the will of God, the ship quickened her way. We shot past a great rock which, minutes before, we seemed doomed to hit upon.

With God's help, we had rounded Cape Deseado. Once by it, we took in all of our sails. We no longer needed them. The wind and the currents carried us forward at such a rate three men were required to control the whipstaffe. Within six hours we were twenty-five leagues up the strait.

By then, too, night was upon us and the master, who knew every cove and inch of the shore perfectly, brought the ship into quiet water where we moored her to trees, due our lack of anchors and sound cables. There we remained for nine days, or until 20 October, in an effort to renew and refresh ourselves. The seamen, in particular, were in sad plight. Their muscles and sinews were so stiff and sore they scarce could move about; their flesh was as the flesh of dead men. Many of them were so infested with lice that the vermin, in clusters as large and larger than peas, were nested beneath the very skin.

On 21 October we once more got underway, not daring to linger longer on account of the state of our victuals. We had chosen a time to put forth when the weather was reasonably calm and settled. But before nightfall the wind, coming from out the west-northwest, had risen to a shrieking gale. We had no choice. We had to go forward through the hell-dark of the night. Fortunately for us, though, Captain Davis, when first we passed through the strait, had made such a complete and accurate chart of every twisting and turning in it, as well as marking the site of each and every dangerous rock, that although the strait in various places is not above a league in breadth he and the master guided us safely during the hours of that awful night.

On 25 October we arrived off the Island of Penguins. In the certainty we would be able to take as many of the birds as we wished, Captain Cotton, the lieutenant, myself, and certain others put off in the ship's boat and reached, without difficulty, the island. Mooring our boat close-in, we went ashore, slew a considerable number of penguins and had a part of them loaded into the boat when, without warning of any sort, a storm arose. Our boat, and before our very eyes, was swamped and sank. Captain Cotton and the lieutenant, without hesitation, leaped into the icy waters and after great effort, and even greater discomfort, recovered our boat. The birds, though, were lost. But even with our boat back, we were still not safe. We were forced to row for our very lives in order to get back aboard. Despite our efforts, we owed no small part of our salvation to Captain Davis and the master. Endangering both the ship and themselves, they remained hove-to until we arrived.

Once on board, we helped to put out the foresail and get the ship underway. Two days later we cleared the strait. Three days after that, 30 October, we were lying off the island which has so many penguins and is but three leagues to the southward of Port Desire. Once again we sent the boat ashore. This time, there were no mishaps. It returned laden, not only with birds, but with eggs as well. The men who had been with the boat reported to us that there were so many nesting penguins on the isle that one could scarcely put his foot down without stepping on an egg. They declared that a ship could be laden with the fowls and their eggs. Having been told this, Captain Davis at once appointed a party consisting of Charles Parker, Edward Smith, and twenty others, which party he ordered to go ashore. They would remain on the island, slaying and drying the meat of penguins, while he and the remainder of the company took the ship to Port Desire. Once the ship was safely in harbour, only a few men would stay in her. The others, by ship's boat, would return to the island to be with the others already there. In this way, the captain had in mind, not only to lay up a goodly store of penguin meat but to conserve what victuals were still aboard.

The captain's reasoning seemed sound. However, Parker and Smith, and a few others, did not see it as such. They were remembering that it was there that they had once conspired to slay the captain and all who were loyal to him. This led them to suspect it might be a plan devised by the captain, which plan would serve two purposes. First, it would provide the captain with revenge;

second, it would decrease the size of the company to the extent there might be victuals enough to see the remainder safely home.

When told of their suspicions and subsequent discontent, Captain Davis used these words in a speech to them:

"I understand your fear for your safety. It is but your guilty consciences at work, and that I do not find difficult to understand. But what truly puzzles me is why you should think me bloodthirsty. That grieves me. It grieves me because, to my mind, it can mean only that you are measuring me, and therefore judging me, against yourselves. I have wronged none of you, at least not knowingly. If there be among you one single man who believes, in his heart, that I have injured him in any way, I would have that man speak out. Let him accuse me of the wrongs I am supposed to have done. The entire company knows, and knows well, that in this very place certain of you plotted to murder me and the master—without cause, as God knows. No punishment was meted out to you. You were forgiven. Now, as of this moment, I have the feeling I might not be too far wrong were I to accuse certain of you of once more being up to some evil. But I do not fear you. God has reduced your number to where you are no longer a threat. That being so, there are things I would tell you: Until now, I have suffered you, not out of any love for you, but for the sake of your master, the general. I hereby promise, and more, I swear before the Almighty Himself, that I will continue to endure you until we are safely back in England. Between now and then I will not use you unfairly in any way. Once in England, though, I promise you that Master Cavendish shall hear of this. But you shall have proper and fair hearing. I swear I will not try to prejudice the general or anyone else against you. I will not seek revenge of any kind.

"And now, as of this present moment, I will not command a single one of you to go onto the isle. The decision I leave to each of you. Any man who would rather stay on the ship, may stay. He has only to raise his hand."

Ten men, which number included Parker and Smith, spoke up and said they would prefer remaining on the ship. The other ten went, and willingly, onto the isle. The remainder of us took the ship to Port Desire and to a place the master had spied out when we were last there. It had a sandy bottom so at the high of the tide we ran the *Desire* aground, lay out our one precious anchor to seaward, and ran mooring lines ashore, fastening them to stakes we had driven deeply into the ground. Thus secured, the ship gave us no trouble or worry during our stay.

On 3 November our boat with wood, water, and as many men as was felt she could safely carry, left for the isle of penguins. She did not get there. Overladen, she rode so low her men became alarmed that she might be swamped so they put back. Weather prevented another attempt being made before 6 November. On that occasion, nine men, Parker, Smith, Townsend, Purpet, and five others, expressed a desire to go to the island—but not by boat. Instead, they said they would walk down the shore until they were opposite the isle. As the isle lay less than a mile from the mainland, the boat could pick them up and ferry them across. When they took their plan to the captain, he offered no objection, saying they could do as they pleased. He advised them, though, to go well armed. He reminded the men that, while no savages had been sighted, that was not to say there were not plenty of them about.

Parker and Smith, and indeed all of them, scoffed at the danger. In jest, they said that if savages appeared it would be the savages, and not they, who would find themselves being devoured. They explained their reason for wishing to go along the shore by saying the land was overrun by deer and ostriches. During the course of their three-league walk they hoped to take some of each. And so it was that Parker and his friends departed by the land route at the same time as the ship's boat put off, by sea, for the isle. The boat reached the isle without mishap. We never saw or heard of the nine men again. What became of them we do not know, though we suspected they were killed and eaten by cannibals. However, when we recalled that, for the most part, the missing men had belonged to that portion of our company who had conspired to murder the captain and all those loyal to him, we had little difficulty seeing, in their disappearance, the judgement of the Lord.

On 11 November all of the company with the exception of Captain Davis, the master, myself, and five others were on the isle. Those of us still on the ship were busying ourselves with various tasks when, and as though out of nowhere, a great multitude of savages appeared on the shore. Their behaviour was most extraordinary. Not only did they keep leaping up and down and uttering hideous cries, but they also kept throwing handfuls of dust into the air. Some, we noticed, were wearing masks shaped like the faces of dogs.

There was never any doubt these people meant us harm. This was proven when, getting to windward of the ship, they set the bushes afire. No harm was done the *Desire*. The truth is, she was never in danger. But the dense clouds of stinking smoke which drifted over her had us gasping for breath. To discourage them, we fired our arquebuses at them. One was hit in the thigh. When that happened all of them fled and we saw them no more.

There is a river at Port Desire. While we were there, the captain and the master thought they should explore it so, in the ship's boat, they went up it for about twenty miles. At that point the water shallowed and they gave up the venture and returned to the ship. Meantime, the men who were on the isle were killing a vast number of penguins and attempting to cure their meat. The penguin, a truly remarkable bird—it is as much and more at home in the water than on land, can dive and swim faster beneath the surface than the smelt it lives upon—sustained us, and sustained us very well, all of the time we were at Port Desire. Easy to take as they have only stumps of wings and cannot fly, their size is about double that of a duck, their flesh equally as good. Without them, I do not know what we would have done. Of course, we varied our fare with other birds and the meat of young seals. Too, and this was most fortunate, we found growing there a herb well-known to seamen and called scurvy-grass. This herb we fried in train oil, along with penguin eggs, and ate it with relish. It did marvels for us, curing us of our swellings and restoring us to health as perfect as we had enjoyed upon our leaving England.

By the latter part of December, we estimated that no fewer than 20,000 penguins had been slain and their meat dried. The quality of the dried meat was causing us concern as we were short on salt, having only that which the captain, the master, and I had made from seawater. From the very time of our arrival, we had been taking seawater and putting it into depressions in the rocks so it would evaporate, leaving its salt behind it. It was a slow and tedious process which required six days.

As events were to prove, we should have worked both longer and more diligently at our salt-making. However, we were growing impatient to be gone so, on 22 December we unmoored the *Desire* and sailed her to the penguins' isle in order that we might take aboard the cured meat. Not too unexpectedly, the tides—they are very wicked by the isle—hindered us greatly in our efforts to get the meat from shore to ship. Indeed Captain Davis, who was labouring as though he were a common seaman, almost lost his life in the process. Only the skill of the master saved him. In the end, and after two days of effort, we gave up and left a third of the birds on the island. Without further ado, we raised our sails, and, on the night of 22 December we departed, shaping our course for the coast of Brazil.

No sooner were we at sea than Captain Davis was seeing to it that a most careful listing was made of all our victuals. When this was done he concluded that, by strict portioning, we had enough to sustain us for six months, by which time we should be back in England, even though our progress would be slowed by the sorry state of our sails and rigging. His ruling on the victuals was that each man should have the following weekly allowance: five ounces meal; nine spoonfuls of oil; one-half pint of peas. Besides those regular items of ship's fare, each mess of four would receive, per day, five penguins. Our water, too, would be carefully guarded. Each mess of four would get six measured quarts of it a day.

It must be said that we did quite well on what had been allotted us, and on 30 January we arrived by the Isle of Placentia in Brazil, a place we had been at on the outward voyage. Not daring to go close in on account of the shoals known to exist, we lay well out. There we remained until night, at which time Captain Davis, using the ship's boat, landed twenty-four men. His plan was that, at first light, they would enter the small settlement on the island, surprise its Portuguese inhabitants, and take from them all the victuals in the place. Everything went as planned. That is, so far as taking the village was concerned. They entered the place at sun up, but found only burned out houses. All the inhabitants had left, leaving behind them only their gardens. The gardens yielded certain fruits and roots and with these our men had to be content. They took quantities of them and returned to the ship.

But while he had been ashore, our captain had taken note of a fine creek where he thought the ship might lie concealed and in safety so, no sooner was he back aboard than we were working the *Desire* in to the shore. We finally, after much sounding and feeling our way, brought her into the creek and moored her to trees. It was fine place for us to be. There was plenty of sweet water and the deserted gardens were but three miles away. Of equal importance, there was an abundance of wood which was needed, not alone for cooking, but so the coopers could fashion new hoops for our casks. Our casks were, like most everything else on the ship, in bad repair. While there, too, Captain Davis was determined that we do all we could to mend our sails and rigging. Therefore, though this need hardly be said, our stay there was not a time for resting but rather a time for working. Each of us, from sun up to sun down, laboured at his appointed task. Always, too, we kept guard against possible attack. Parties going ashore went in number and well armed. However, despite all precautions ordered there were some who grew careless. Thus it was that when the enemy struck, a number of our men were taken by surprise.

However, we had been given warning of a sort. Though it was of a most unusual nature, I would we had paid more heed to it. It was like this: The night of 4 February many of our men had strange dreams. In the morning, they reported on their dreams with one man saying to another: I dreamed that thou wert slain. Almost without exception the man thus spoken to replied: I dreamed that thou wert also slain. Very soon the story had travelled throughout the ship. Upon its reaching the ears of Captain Davis, he also admitted to having had strange and disturbing dreams. He, therefore, issued the most strict orders. All men going ashore, he said, should go well armed and keep their wits about them. Men working should do so only while other men were standing guard.

His orders were carried out, in every detail, until ten of the clock in the morning. Then a company of fifteen men who were ashore, working in the woods, found the heat unbearable. They ceased their labours and, retiring to some rocks near the shore, lighted a fire and prepared themselves a meal of cassava root, which is plentiful on the island. It was so quiet, so peaceful, that when they had eaten they lolled about on the ground in complete disregard of the captain's orders. Some went to sleep. A few stripped and went bathing in the sea. Not a piece was primed. Not a match was lighted.

Suddenly there appeared, as though out of nowhere, a large body of Portuguese and Indians. They fell upon our men, slaying all but two of them. Those two, though one was sorely wounded, escaped into the woods.

Aboard, we heard the shots. Realizing our men were being attacked, we landed to try to succour them. We were, of course, too late. We found them dead and stripped of their clothing. Their bodies were laid in a neat row, face-up, and near them the Portuguese had planted a cross. Shortly afterwards, we spied two very large pinnaces which we surmised had been sent from the River January to take us. We had no intention of allowing them to do that, but their very presence had us in a bad way. The thirteen men we had lost had reduced our number, from the seventy-five it was to begin with, to a mere twenty-seven. Our casks, many of which were still not in condition to hold water, would allow us to take no more than eight tons of the precious liquid aboard. To put to sea with no more water than that would be inviting death from thirst.

However, we had a more immediate worry. For lack of cables and anchors, we were moored to the very shore. The soldiers sent from the River January vastly outnumbered us. What, we asked ourselves, was to prevent those soldiers from assaulting us, and overcoming us, where we lay. Thus we were presented with two choices, each a hard one. We could unmoor the *Desire,* put to sea, and run the risk of dying from thirst. Or we could remain where we were and invite an even more certain death at the hands of the Portuguese. Differently worded, the choice was really into whose hands we would prefer to fall: The hands of men whose cruelties we had already witnessed, or the hands of God Whose mercies we had before experienced. We chose the latter.

On the 6 February, after first putting in readiness our ordnance and our smaller pieces as well, we cast off the mooring lines and began working our way out of the channel. Aided by a small gale which chose that time to blow, we gained the open sea. Now the Isle of Placentia, this we knew from the outward voyage, lies some thirty leagues westward of Cabo Frio. By skirting the shoreline, we reached the vicinity of the cape. But when we tried to round the cape in order to set course to the northward, we were vexed, beyond all reason, by contrary winds and cross-winds so that for three whole weeks we could go nowhere. During those wasted days our water diminished to the place where we were in such distress that some of our men were actually suggesting we go to Baya and submit to the Portuguese. This idea Captain Davis refused to entertain. Finally, God came to our assistance. He sent such a deluge of rain our thirst was slaked. Too, we replenished our butts to such extent we could proceed in comfort.

We held course to the northward, but as we neared the Equator the sun's heat increased. When it did, our cured but poorly salted penguins began to rot. In doing so, there bred in the corrupt flesh a loathsome and ugly worm, measuring about an inch in length. These worms increased mightily. Very soon the entire ship was overrun by them, and there was not one single thing the wicked creatures did not try to devour. Excepting iron. First, they attacked our scanty store of victuals. More, they nibbled at our clothing, boots, shoes, hats, shirts, and stockings. They even gnawed at the ship's timbers. Naturally, we battled them. But the more of them we killed the more did they seem to multiply. Then, finally, they began to attack us. When one of us would lie down, either to sleep or simply to rest, the hideous vermin would crawl over us, nibbling at our flesh. Their bite was as vicious as that of a mosquito.

We were indeed in woeful state. But worse things were in store. After we had crossed the Equator, our men began to fall sick of such a monstrous disease I doubt its like has ever before been seen. At its first onslaught, a man's ankles would become sore and swollen. Working upward, two days later it would have reached their breasts, making their breathing difficult and a torture. Then it would reverse course and descend into the cod and the yard [genitals] of the victim. Both would swell enormously, and the pain would be so great the man could not bear to stand, lie or, particularly, move about. Some of the stricken men went mad from pain and grief.

During those darkest of days, our captain knew anguish of soul, but he exhorted all of us to accept our misfortunes as God's chastisement, the same time he beseeched us to pray to Him for deliverance. The master, through all of this, remained in both good health and spirits, even though men died until there were but sixteen of us left alive. Among those sixteen there were five only of us in sufficient health to haul on a line. These included Captain Davis, whom the disorder shunned entirely, the master who was affected very slightly; Captain Cotton and myself, each of us swollen but able to get about, and a boy who, like the captain, remained unaffected. Upon the five of us fell all the labour of the ship. We made and took in sail; we tended the whipstaffe. We did our best. But it was not so good but that our sails became torn and shredded, while the entire ship became woefully dirty and noisome. Not the least of the things we had to endure were the cries of pain and the lamentations of the sick.

Thus as wanderers upon the sea, on 11 June 1593, it pleased God to guide us into Bearhaven in Ireland where we ran the *Desire* ashore. There, the Irishmen helped us moor her so she would float and be safe. For their slender pains they charged our captain the sum of £10. Within five days Captain Davis, leaving the master and four others to tend the ship, found passage for himself and the remainder of the company to England in a fishing boat out of Padstow in Cornwall. In this manner, and by God's mercy, our small remnant was preserved. Thus ended the voyage.

When he arrived back in England after his first voyage, Cavendish was rich and idolized by the people. In three years he was again on the verge of bankruptcy. He decided to make another voyage around the world and got together a fleet. He authorized for supplies the sum of £1,500, giving the money to two rogues to carry out his wishes. The would-be suppliers, and the money, promptly disappeared. As a result, Cavendish put to sea in a fleet that was low in provisions and had rotting sails and cordage.

Cavendish no longer seemed a rational man. He quarrelled with all his officers. In the Strait of Magellan he allowed sick men to be put ashore to die of hunger and exposure. In that same strait he decided he could reach the Americas by way of the Cape of Good Hope. When Captain Davis made it clear that the idea was a foolish one, Cavendish sulked. Quitting the strait, he sailed back up the coast of Brazil, where, in the hopes he could replenish his supplies, he ranged northwards, raiding settlements along the coast. At other times, he raided and burned plantations with, seemingly, no other reason than his own amusement. But Cavendish's luck had run out. Everything went wrong. The towns he tried to raid were both well alerted and well defended. His other ships, or so he believed, had deserted him. He died at sea.

The voyage of

The Delight

as told by William Magoths

Nothing is known about William Magoths who wrote this narrative of the *Delight*'s voyage to the Strait of Magellan. As he appears to have been an educated person, we may assume he was a gentleman-soldier engaged in the venture.

John Chidley, leader of the expedition, was a wealthy man. A gambler by nature, he was one of the merchants from the West of England who backed John Davis on his second voyage in search of the Northwest Passage, and he must have been generous. Davis gave his name to a cape at the southern entrance to Hudson Strait. It is still called Cape Chidley.

The writer-historian K. R. Andrews describes Chidley as a young gentleman of good family, born in 1565. Inspired by Drake's voyage around the world, he decided to become a privateer himself. Unfortunately, he never progressed beyond the amateur stage. Generous he was; shrewd he was not. Andrews informs us that to outfit the expedition of which the *Delight* was a part, he pledged practically his entire fortune. The expedition is said to have cost over £10,000, an enormous sum for those days. Of course, he had partners, but he was the main shareholder.

The voyage of the *Delight* is one of the horror stories of the sea and, for this reason, is included in this collection of Hakluyt's tales.

On 5 August 1589, Master John Chidley, of Chidley in the County of Devon, with Master Paul Wheele and Captain Andrew Mericke, set forth from Plymouth with three tall ships and two pinnaces, the pinnaces being of fourteen and fifteen tons. Master Chidley, our general, was in a ship of 300 tons called the *Wildman* which had for her master Benjamin Wood and her company consisted of 180 persons. In the second ship, the *White Lion* of 340 tons, there were 140 persons; Master Paul Wheele [Master Polewhele] was her captain, John Ellis her master. The third ship, and the one which I, William Magoths, was in, was the *Delight* of Bristol. Our captain was Master Andrew Mericke, our master was Robert Burnet. In all, our company numbered ninety-one persons, some of whom were boys.

The voyage was intended for the South Sea by way of the Strait of Magellan and, having passed through the strait, it was in Master Chidley's mind that we range the coast of Chili. Master Chidley had so planned our course that we would, upon leaving England, drop southward to Cape Blanco on the Barbary coast of Africa, after which we would sail westward toward Brazil.

Our ships had no difficulty keeping in touch with each other until we had reached Cape Blanco, which stands in 20° north latitude. There while we lay offshore, various of our men went onto the land but found nothing to interest them greatly so that when they had come back aboard we departed toward Brazil. Twelve days later, during the night, the *Delight* became separated from the fleet. However, we held to the pre-arranged course and, upon raising the coast of Brazil we sailed southward along it, passing by the mouth of the River Plate and finally arriving in Port Desire which lies in 48° south latitude. But it would be an untruth to say we reached that place without difficulty. Besides our still not having sighted the other ships of the fleet, and the usual tempests, sixteen of our men had died of sundry causes, including disease.

Upon reaching Port Desire, our company was so weary and our ship in such need of repair, we decided to remain there for a time. But we did not idle the days away. A watch was kept in the hope Master Chidley and the other ships would appear; we graved the the *Delight* and repaired her as best we could. We replenished our water from two springs which we found upon the land. Too, seals being plentiful we killed a number of them for their meat. At the end of seventeen days we left Port Desire and, sailing southward, we entered the mouth of the strait about 1 January. Some leagues into it, we came to the place which is called Penguin Island, so named for its multitude of birds. We slew and salted several hogsheads of penguins but, alas, we discovered that even when salted their flesh will not keep for long.

It was while we were lying off Penguin Island that we suffered a great misfortune. A boat with fifteen men was sent to the island to bring back a last, and final, supply of the birds. While they were gone from us a sudden spell of thick, foul weather descended upon us. The viciousness of the storm was such we lost two anchors. And never again did we see either the boat or any of its fifteen men.

Departing from Penguin Island, we passed farther into the strait and, in due course, arrived at Port Famine. When first erected, by the Spaniards, to guard the strait, it had been called El Ciudad de Rey Filipe—The City of King Philip. We found it deserted, except for a lone Spaniard who told us he had lived by himself for six years, supporting himself with his caliver. All of his more than 400 companions, he said, had perished of famine or disease. At Port Famine, and because we had lost our only boat back by Penguin Island, it was decided we should build another one from boards taken from chests aboard our ship. The boat was built. When it was finished, nine men went in it to the north shore of the strait, for there savages had been showing themselves and waving white skins at us, which gestures we took to be signs of friendship.

However, when seven of our men had been enticed ashore, the wild people fell upon and slew them all. The two who had remained in the boat did not suffer this fate; they returned to us alive. After this show of treachery we would have nothing further to do with the savages. We even moved our ship back to the road which lies to the eastward of Port Famine and there we refreshed ourselves with mussels; we also took in fresh water and wood. The wood and the water aboard, we made sail and passed to the westward until we were as many as ten leagues beyond Cape Froward. But then the winds and the currents became so much in our disfavour there were occasions when, despite the greatest of efforts on our part, we would be driven back more in two hours than we could gain in headway in eight. For a full six weeks we battled against them, and during that time no fewer than thirty-eight of our men died either through injury or sickness. As well, we lost two of our three anchors. Little wonder then that members of the company were saying aloud we should turn back and give up the action. There were threats of mutiny. Finally, it became evident that if we remained longer in the strait there would not be enough men left alive to work the ship so, on 14 February 1590, we turned homeward.

We passed out of the strait and turned northward, going by the mouth of the River Plate and continuing up the coast of Brazil until we arrived by the Island of San Sebastion. There we spied a Portuguese ship of eighty tons lying at anchor in a road. Upon seeing us, and believing we meant to take them, the Portuguese weighed their anchors and ran. However, all they managed to do was run their ship aground between the island and the mainland. We came near to being as unfortunate as they. First, we had no decent boat—indeed that same lack of a ship's boat kept us from so much as getting ashore to renew our water supply; second, a sudden spell of foul weather had us putting out to sea for greater safety, for we did not want to run aground as had the Portuguese.

All things being as they were, we had no choice other than to shape our course for the Cape Verde Islands, which we did, placing our trust in God, for we were in extreme misery with men continuing to die. Our fortunes did not improve as various things prevented our touching the Cape Verdes, the Azores, or the Canaries so that, in truth, the first land we met with was the Isle of Aldernay [in the English Channel]. By then there were but six men still alive and, the master, his two mates, and all of the chief mariners having died, we six had difficulty working the ship. On that account, the best we could do was bring her to an anchorage eight miles to the westward of Cherbourg on the Normandy coast.

But the very next day, which was 30 August, foul weather beset us and caused the *Delight* to drag her one remaining anchor and she drove onto the rocks. The Normans ashore saw this happen; they could have saved our ship by supplying us with another anchor. Alas, they were more interested in seeing our ship split so they could profit from the wreck. When the ship began to break up, we made our way safely to shore. Within a few days after this final misfortune, four of us found passage to England in a bark of Weymouth. The other two men, one being a Briton [Breton] and one a Portuguese, chose to remain in Normandy.

The names of the six of us who survived the voyage are, William Magoths of Bristol; Richard Bush; John Reade; Richard Hodgkins of Westbury near Bristol; Gabriel Valeros, a Portuguese; Peter, a Briton.

• • •

A petition made by certain of the company of the *Delight* unto the master of the said *Delight,* Robert Burnet, in the Strait of Magellan on 12 February 1589:

"We have thought it best to bring to you, our master, what we consider to be our just grievances. It is known to us that Captain Hawlse and your mate, Walter Street, have this very day taken into the captain's cabin victuals, chiefly bread and butter, which were intended for the whole company and not just for those in their own mess. It seems then that they would rather the rest of us starve than that we be kept in strength and good health. It is also known that upon this day they have taken into the captain's cabin swords, muskets, and calivers. We do not know for certain why they do this, but from words which have been heard by certain of us we judge they may well have in their minds to bring about your death.

"With all of these matters troubling us sorely, we all humbly implore you, as our master, to consider the following items: First, we beg you to recall that we have already lost many men: sixteen died on the way hence; fifteen were lost in the boat, during the sudden storm, by Penguin Island. Another seven were slain by the wild people near Port Famine. Our carpenter, a most necessary member of our company, is among those who are dead. Then there is the sorry condition of our ship. It is in sad disrepair and we have but one anchor left us.

"Aside from the above listed calamities, we would remind you of the manner in which you have been overruled, disobeyed, insulted, and disgraced by your mate, Street, to say naught of the conduct of the captain toward you. We also warn you that these same persons are conspiring to see you dead and if, God forbid, that should occur, we should be in greater peril still than we now are. We beseech you, therefore, to weigh well, not alone the dangers to yourself, but the great want of necessities within this ship. We have but six sailors who are capable and whom we dare trust. We have a single anchor. No boat. No carpenter. No chirurgeon. There is a grievous shortage of rope, pitch, treenails, bolts, and planks. We have viewed our provisions and found that, in our opinion, we have at very most a five-month supply of them in the form of bread, meal, grits, and peas. Of meats we have a three-month supply. There are three hogsheads of wine and ten gallons of aquavitae. The latter, as you may well know, is in such short supply it is being denied the sick men.

"We have, it is true, four hogsheads of cider and twenty-one flitches of bacon. But of the bacon only three sides have been put aside for the use of the company. The remaining eighteen have been seized by Hawlse and Street for, or so we believe, their own use. The same two have also seized for themselves seventeen pots of butter, certain cheeses, and a hogshead of bread. Sweetmeats which were intended for the comfort of the sick are being withheld. And even as they eat well and even grow fat while others starve, they make a great pretence of grieving at the small allowance of food given those of us who have to labour, even going so far as to declare they deny themselves so that more might be available for us.

"Weigh all of these matters well, Master Burnet, for while you are considering them there are still other things which we would bring to your attention, among them the great long time we have been in the Strait of Magellan. No fewer than eight times have we fought our way westward to Cape Froward and beyond. Eight times we have been driven back by tempests. Too, there will soon be added dangers for, as you shall have noticed, the fogs and the mists are on the increase. They will worsen as the southern winter approaches. Had we so much as a decent boat in which to seek fair harbours to lie in it would be a great advantage but we have, instead, a poor affair fashioned from the boards of men's sea-chests. We dare not put off in it but keep it aboard to be used only in the most dire of extremities. Considering all of the things conspiring against us, we are of the firm opinion we can never get through the Strait of Magellan and into the South Sea this season. Even if we did, by some miracle, get through we are so short of necessities it would avail us little. We could all of us perish. The truth, Master Burnet, is this: We have scarcely enough victuals to risk sailing for home.

"Again we humbly beg that you have due regard for your own safety and the safety of those of us still alive in order that we may, by God's help, get back to England and not die here in this harsh land among a wild and savage people. To stay longer in this place can result only in further loss and decay, both to ourselves and to our ship. Should we turn back now, it might please God to have us find the fifteen men, and our boat, which were lost by Penguin Island, though we well know that Captain Hawlse and your mate, Street, would rather these men remain lost, for, to have them found, would mean sharing our victuals with them. True, there would be a sharing. But should we put our trust in God, and all of us pray and love one another, the Almighty would not forsake us; instead He would send us sufficient food to see us safely home.

"Last, we would point out to you certain things having to do with the conduct of our captain. We ask you to remember how, as we were taking on water at Port Famine and three of our men, the boatswain, the hooper, and William Magoths were ashore, the Captain did haloo to them and order them to come aboard with all haste. Then to those of us who stood near him he said these words, 'This voyage will not be delayed for the sake of two or three men. They come at once or we leave them.'

"His words did not really surprise us, for it was known to us that he was, at that very moment, carrying a pistol under his gown, which pistol was intended for the murdering of Andrew Stoning and William Combe. This we learned from the mouth of his own servant, William Martin. The said William Martin confided to Richard Hungate and Emanuel Dornel, friends of his, that the captain had even made known to him his evil intentions, and that upon his doing so he, William Martin, had gone down on his knees before the captain, and begged for one whole hour that the men's lives be spared.

"Another item we would mention, one you yourself have knowledge of, occurred as we were watering for the second time by Port Famine. You, Master Burnet, were in the gunroom with Thomas Browne, the master gunner, and his mate, William Frier. Hawlse came to you and asked your opinion as to whether or not a party of men, for some purpose he did not define, should be sent to Port Famine. Without allowing you to reply, Thomas Browne spoke out boldly against it, saying that should a gale arise we might very well lose the men at Port Famine which was all of two leagues from where the ship lay.

"To that, Hawlse replied that should they be lost it would be of small consequence as he had chosen men we could do without. He then gave the names of those men whose lives meant so little to him. They were as follows: Emmanuel Dornel, Richard Hungate, Paul Carie, John Davis, Gabriel Valerosa the Portuguese, and Peter the Briton, as well as the Spaniard we found at Port Famine when first we called there.

"Thus we end this petition, desiring only that God see us back in safety to our own native country. In witness whereof we have signed our names:

Thomas Browne, gunner; John Morice; etc., etc."

The aquavitae mentioned in the petition was probably brandy or whisky of some sort.

It is not known what became of the *Delight's* first captain, Andrew Mericke. He probably died and was replaced by a lieutenant.

The petition was included in this account of the voyage of the *Delight* because it tells us a great deal about conditions aboard sixteenth- and seventeenth-century ships. For the between-deck seamen it must have been a fair imitation of hell. The petitioners were no doubt telling the truth when they spoke of the captain and the mate keeping arms in the cabin and taking more than their share of the food. Such action was not the exception but the rule. Two decades later Henry Hudson found himself charged with keeping victuals in his cabin while his men starved. After he had been set adrift in Hudson Bay, his cabin was indeed found to be well stocked with food.

And now for a last word about Master John Chidley: after the *Delight* had become separated from the other ships, Chidley, with the remainder of his fleet, proceeded on and reached the coast of Guiana (Guyana). There, an epidemic of some sort hit them. Chidley, the captain of the *White Lion,* Master Polewhele, and numerous seamen from all of the ships died. All thought of trying to reach the Strait of Magellan was given up by the survivors. One by one the ships limped home. The *Wildman,* Chidley's ship, turned up a year later. Her crew had taken her to Trinidad and lingered there until they were again in good health.

GLOSSARY

Ahull or Lying Ahull

When ahull, a ship has all sail taken in; her tiller might be lashed and she is probably being driven before a gale or tempest.

Armada

A fleet of Spanish galleons. The fleet sent against England in 1588 was called the Invincible Armada.

Astrolabe

A small, brass, circular instrument used for determining latitude. Of ancient origin, the astrolabe was probably invented by the Arabs.

Between-decks

The space immediately below the waist-deck and the poops. It housed the guns and the seamen.

Binnacle

A receptacle for a ship's compass; in the sixteenth and seventeenth centuries, generally a wooden box affair, so as to be non-magnetic and therefore not affect the compass needle.

Bitts

A pair of posts protruding from the ship's deck. Used for fastening cables, stays, sheets, etc.

Block

A device consisting of one or more grooved pulleys mounted in a casing.

Boatswain or Bosun

The one man, other than the ship's master, who was permitted to carry a whistle, probably because the bosun gave more commands than anyone else except the master; to summon all hands, if necessary, in case of a sudden emergency. Was charged with keeping the ship's rigging, cables, anchors, etc., in repair.

Bonnets and Drabblers

Strips of sailcloth that could be attached to the lower edges of the mainsails to increase the spread.

Bowsprit

A mast, or spar, projecting outward and upward from the ship's head. Had one yard, and one sail, the spritsail.

Busse

A type of ship, a two-masted fishing vessel.

Cable

A thick, usually three-strand rope by which the anchor was weighed or dropped. The term "cable's length" meant 100 fathoms or 600 feet.

Calendar (Old Style)

The Julian Calendar. Was replaced in 1582 by the Gregorian Calendar which was based on the solar year. The Gregorian Calendar corrected the Julian year which was out one day in every 128 years.

Caliver

A type of musket.

Capstan

Upright device with holes through which bars could be thrust. Used to bring in or drop anchor.

Caravel

Small, light, fast ship of the sixteenth and seventeenth centuries, chiefly Spanish or Portuguese. Carried both sails and oars.

Cartography

Map drawing.

Chirurgeon

Archaic name for surgeon.

Chronometer
A clock that will keep accurate time at sea, thereby enabling navigators to determine longitude, i.e., how far to the east or west they are of the prime meridian at Greenwich, England.

Clinker
A ship constructed in a certain way: the strakes overlap each other.

Cosmography
The description and mapping of the general features of the earth and/or the universe.

Cross-staffe
A large, rather cumbersome instrument fashioned in the form of a cross. Used to determine latitude.

Crowsnest
A cage high on the mainmast for use by the lookout.

Darts
Light spears that can be thrown. The Eskimo darts mentioned by Frobisher's men were most likely harpoons.

Deckhouse
A house-like structure, flat topped or decked, built on the upper deck of a ship. The poops and forecastle of the early ships were, in a very real sense, deckhouses.

Doublet
A close-fitting garment, with or without sleeves. Somewhat similar to some modern vests and/or jackets.

Falconet
A small cannon. Often used as a signal gun.

Flieboat or Flyboat
A shallow-draught, flat-bottomed vessel designed for use in coastal waters.

Footrope
The footrope mentioned in "The Last Voyage of Cavendish" should not be confused with what was generally referred to as the footropes. There was a vast difference between the two. The one that broke on the *Desire* was apparently a rope attached to the bottom of the mainsail to strengthen it and keep the sail from tearing. The "real" footropes were lines strung, in loops, along the yards. The seamen stood in the loops when furling the sails or doing other work, hence the term footropes.

Forecastle
Deckhouse in forepart of ship. Used during sixteenth century mainly for storing cordage, etc.

Foremast
The most forward upright mast of a ship. The bowsprit was farther forward but it projected outward and upward from the beak of the ship.

Friseland
Name given to Greenland by Martin Frobisher.

Galleon
Sixteenth-century galleons were shorter but much, much higher than were the galleys of the same period. The enormous Spanish ships of war were usually of the galleon type.

Galley
(1) A ship's kitchen. (2) A single-decked, often very long and large vessel having both sails and oars but usually propelled by oars manned by slaves or criminals. Used as a ship of war until circa 1600.

Goldfiners
Archaic term for persons who could extract gold from ore. Probably goldsmiths.

Hawser
A small cable used mainly for mooring a ship to a dock or other objects ashore.

Hogshead
Large wooden cask, or butt, used to store water, wine, meat, etc. See also Tonnage of a Ship.

Iron Pyrites
A common mineral that because of its lustre is often mistaken for gold ore, and hence is known as fool's gold.

Land of Desolation
John Davis' name for Greenland.

Larboard
Archaic term for port. That which is to your left as you face the bow of the ship.

London Coast
Name given to part of west Greenland by John Davis.

Maincourses
The lower, largest sails on the main and foremasts.

Mainmast
The tallest mast of the ship. Located in central part of ship; had two yards and two sails.

Mainpoop
The lower and larger of the two poops of a ship that had two poop decks. The upper poop rested partly on the mainpoop with the remainder of it hanging out over the stern.

Mainsail
The lower and larger of the mainmast's sails. Its counterpart on the foremast was known as the fore mainsail or fore-course.

Master
The master was the man who really "worked" the ship. Was second in command to the captain, who might not be a man with sea experience. Like the boatswain, he carried a whistle.

Masts
Stout, upright poles which carried the yards and sails of the ship.

Merchants Coast
Part of Greenland coast, so named by Davis because the natives were so eager to trade.

Mizzen Mast
Small mast protruding upward through the deck of the mainpoop. Had one sail attached to a boom which could be set at any angle.

Mussels
Edible marine bivalves of the family *Mytilidae.*

New Found Land
When spelled this way in the text, it does not refer specifically to Newfoundland but to the whole of America.

Ordnance
Cannon, artillery.

Penquins
Seabirds that cannot fly. Those mentioned in the voyage of Master Hore were the now-extinct great auks.

Piece
A personal weapon and one of the various kinds of muskets: wheelock, matchlock, caliver, snaphaunce.

Pilot
Usually the first mate of the ship who, along with other duties, was responsible for navigating the ship.

Pinnace
A small, one-masted, fleet craft which usually sailed in consort with a larger vessel.

Pizzle
Penis.

Poops
The deckhouses in the after part of the ship. There were usually two with one atop and nearer the stern than the other. They contained, besides the great cabin, the cabins of the officers and the chart-room. The lower, or mainpoop, would probably also have the compass and its binnacle as well as the whipstaffe.

Port
That which is to the left of a person standing facing the bow of the ship.

Prependary
A canon or clergyman who, for a stipend, performed special services for a cathedral.

Pulley
A wheel with a grooved rim for carrying a rope, turning in a frame or block. Used for raising weights and taughtening ropes. A pair of double-grooved pulleys with their rope could increase by four times the power applied.

Ratlines
Small ropes fastened at regular intervals and crosswise of the shrouds. Served as ladders for men going aloft.

Rigging
The term applies chiefly to those ropes that need only to be tightened, mended or replaced from time to time: the shrouds and stays, etc.

Rudder
In the sixteenth and seventeenth centuries, a broad, flat wooden piece hinged to the ship's stern. Its function was to enable the ship to be steered.

Sandglass or Seaglass
A glass instrument, containing sand, used for measuring time. The seaglasses (sand-glasses) on sixteenth-century ships took one half hour to run. A watch consisted of eight glasses.

Scurvy
A condition caused by lack of Vitamin C. A major cause of illness and death on ships of the period.

Sea Unicorn
A narwhal, a sea mammal often mistaken by the early sea explorers for the mythical unicorn because of its spirally twisted tusk that protruded from its upper jaw for as much as nine feet. Body length of a male narwhal is around twelve feet.

Sheets
The ropes, or lines, attached to the lower outside corners of both top and mainsails. When the sails were put out, or set, the sheets secured them either to the lower yards or, in the case of the mainsails, to bitts inboard.

Ship's boat
Any of the various small boats which a ship might carry inboard: longboat, light horsemen, dory, dinghy, lifeboat.

Shrouds
Ropes, set in pairs, one on either side of the ship and running upward from the chains, or chainwales, to points high on the masts. They acted as supports for the masts and, with the ratlines, formed ladders for men going aloft.

Spar
A stout pole, especially such as is used for either a mast or a yard of a ship.

Spritsail

The single sail carried by the bowsprit. Its purpose was to act as a counterbalance to the towering poops and so give the ship more stability.

Starboard

That which is to the right of a person standing facing the bow of the ship.

Stays

Ropes strung from high on the masts so that they angled down to the decks where they were secured. The stays kept the masts from bending too far forward or backward.

Strakes

The continuous longitudinal planks of the side of a boat.

Tonnage of a Ship

The ton is a unit of measurement employed to define the size or carrying capacity of a ship. In the sixteenth century it was based on the number of hogsheads of wine that could be stored in the hold, four hogsheads being reckoned as a ton.

Waistdeck

The amidships open deck between the mainpoop and the forecastle. It was also, at times, called the weatherdeck. Much of the ship's work was done in the waist—or, if you will, on the waistdeck.

Whipstaffe

The steering device, a bar attached to the rudder and which entered the ship through an opening in the stern. Ship's wheels did not appear until the early eighteenth century.

Yard

A spar set at right angles to the mast. The yards carried the sails and could be brought around, or veered, so the ship could sail "closer the wind."

BIBLIOGRAPHY

Andrews, K.R., *Elizabethan Privateering* (London: The Cambridge University Press, 1964)

Asher, G.M., *Henry Hudson the Navigator* (London: The Hakluyt Society, 1860)

Blacker, Irwin R., *Hakluyt's Voyages* (New York: The Viking Press, 1965)

Bradford, E.D.S., *Drake* (London: Hodder & Stoughton, 1965)

Charlton, Warwick, *The Second Mayflower Adventure* (Boston: Little, Brown & Company, 1957)

Chatterton, E.K., *Sailing the Seas* (London: Chapman and Hall Ltd., 1931)

Chatterton, E.K., *Ships and Ways of Other Days* (London: Sidgwick & Jackson Ltd., 1913)

Christy, Miller, *Voyages of Foxe and James* (London: Hakluyt Society, 1894)

Encyclopaedia Britannica, particularly Vol. XVII of the 1898 Edition (New York: The Werner Company)

Gibbs, Lewis, *The Silver Circle* (London: J.M. Dent & Sons Ltd., 1963)

Gill, Crispin, *Plymouth, A New History* (Newton Abbot, Devon: David & Charles, 1966)

Gosch, C.A.A., *Danish Arctic Expeditions 1606-1620* (London: The Hakluyt Society, 1897)

Hadfield, Alice M., *Time to Finish the Game* (London: Phoenix House, 1964)

Hakluyt, Richard, *The Principall Navigations, Voiages and Discoveries of the English Nation* (London: J.M. Dent & Sons Ltd., 1908)

Jones, Gwyn, *The Norse Atlantic Saga* (London: Oxford University Press, 1964)

Marx, Robert F., *The Voyage of the Nina II* (Cleveland: The World Publishing Company, 1963)

Mowat, Farley, *Ordeal by Ice* (Toronto: McClelland & Stewart, 1960)

Mowat, Farley, *Westviking* (Toronto: McClelland & Stewart, 1965)

Parks, George Bruner, *Richard Hakluyt & the English Voyages* (New York: Frederick Unger Publishing Co., 1961)

Powys, Llewelyn, *Henry Hudson* (London: John Lane the Bodley Head Ltd., 1927)

Rundall, Thomas, *Narratives of Voyages Toward the North-West* (New York: Burt Franklin)

Southey, Robert, *English Seamen,* Two Volumes (London: Methuen & Co., 1897)

Villiers, Allan, *Give Me a Ship to Sail* (New York: Charles Scribner's Sons, 1958)

Williamson, James A., *Age of Drake* (London: A. & C. Black, Limited, 1938)

Wycherley, George, *Buccaneers of the Pacific* (Indianapolis: The Bobbs-Merrill Co., Inc., 1928)

INDEX